MW00955661

Mastering Small Talk

Building Confidence & Strategies for
Engaging Conversations

Judy Best

Contents

Introduction

Alright, let's be honest. Making small talk used to make me anxious. The butterflies would start when I was in any social situation where I might need to chat. It didn't matter if it was a happy hour with colleagues, a family wedding, or just the checkout line at the grocery store. That panicky voice in my head would go off immediately:

"Don't say something stupid."

"They can tell how awkward you are."

"Quick, look at your phone so nobody talks to you!"

I'd resort to frankly pathetic levels of avoidance to steer clear of casual conversations with anybody outside my familiar circle. I'd beg friends and partners not to abandon me, hover in the outer peripheries of any room with my cell phone, and smile and nod at others near me doing the same. Maybe you can relate to these extreme wallflower tactics.

Sadly, I wasn't even outrageously shy or lacking social skills overall. Within a small group of friends or my professional zone of genius, I morphed into a friendly, articulate person without any struggle. It was only in larger groups where I had to join a conversation already in process or start a conversation with someone standing alone – this was my struggle!

No, my small talk paralysis stemmed from a fear of rejection and judgment from casual strangers. That nagging voice of self-doubt convinced me that any new acquaintance would instantly write me off as "weird" or dislike me when I opened my mouth to make small talk.

So, I just ... didn't. Clamming up became a brutally self-defeating defense mechanism to avoid the embarrassment of someone's fleeting sneer or arched eyebrow of disdain. It was better to fade into the conversational wallpaper and not risk it.

At least, that's where my headspace was stuck for a good long while. This led to me missing out on many potential connections and social opportunities, not to mention dulling my communication skills from sheer lack of practice.

Honestly, it wasn't until challenges arose in my career that I started accepting that my small talk paralysis could no longer be sustained. As a professional responsibility, I'd have to start putting myself out there through all the idle networking and chitchat.

Let me tell you, stepping out of my cozy conversational shell after a lifetime of hiding did NOT come naturally at first. I bombed constantly, muscling through wave after wave of cringe attempts until I started piecing together more positive momentum.

Conquering small talk became my goal, and I worked on it like a job. I did everything, from memorizing a running list of icebreaker topics to practicing conversation openings with myself in the mirror. I forced uncomfortable smiles and eye contact until they began to feel more natural. I studied successful small talkers to try mimicking their seamless charisma.

Let's say it like it is: the early days were rough, but no one exchanges ineffective habits in their life for good without a struggle. I popped a rubber band against my wrist whenever I clammed up or started panicky negative self-talk in the middle of a chat. The stretching and behavioral adjustments caused those old anxious impulses to soften, slowly loosening their death grip on my willpower. I knew I'd embraced my newfound confidence in small talk as I left each event with a smile and several new contacts and friends to connect with in the coming days.

Don't get me wrong; I'm still not about to be tapped as a late-night TV host anytime soon. Making casual small talk remains more of a diligently acquired skillset than an effortless gift for this introvert. But I've leveled up to a more comfortable zone of personal growth:

I'm no longer intimidated by the mere thought of introducing myself to strangers and chatting. Even better, I've discovered the low-key joys of using small talk for momentary connection. I form breezy social threads by swapping jokes with cashiers or complimenting gorgeous shoes on a lady in a store.

It's become a heartening exercise to discover commonalities with folks I'd never cross paths with—a mutual love of sci-fi flicks, the comically relatable hell of family dynamics, whatever. However superficial, these little momentary bonds have surprisingly enriched my day-to-day life.

Purpose of the Book

I'm telling you all this not to brag about moderately okay conversation skills but hopefully to illustrate an important truth. Nobody, and I mean nobody, is "born" excellent at small talk right out of the womb. We all start from different small talk ability levels shaped by our backgrounds and comfort zones.

Some are naturally gifted with an innate ease for casual banter, sure. For the rest of us mere mortals, we must work to eliminate our fears and learn new skills to do the following:

- Initiate ice-breaking conversations gracefully

- Keep topics and questions flowing

- Pick up on verbal/non-verbal social cues

- Balance between making points and active listening

- Not stalling out or overstaying your welcome

It's going to require diligent practice and mindset training. The good news? With the right toolkit of practical strategies and a smidge of self-compassion, damn near anybody can acquire competent-to-excellent small talk skills over time.

That's precisely what this book aims to equip you with—no matter where you're starting from on the communication confidence spectrum. Over the following chapters, we'll outline a comprehensive game plan for tackling the mental and tactical roadblocks holding you back from casual chatting success. If I can do it, so can you!

You'll learn actionable mindset shifts and psychological reframes to overcome issues like social anxiety, fear of rejection, and self-sabotaging internal narratives. Plus, powerful techniques to "deactivate" those harrowing automatic negative thought patterns and replace them with more positive self-talk and self-assurance.

From there, we'll dive into the literal mechanics of small talk—properly introducing yourself, reading body language and tonal cues, and smoothly transitioning between light topics in a conversational flow state. So much of confident mingling comes from rote practice with those basics.

Eventually, we'll layer on more advanced strategies like astute question-asking, recognizing opportunities to deepen conversations, and navigating cultural/environmental nuances—all part of evolving your newfound skills into an adaptable social toolkit.

This book is ultimately about becoming unflustered and present in casual social scenarios. You'll gain a formidable arsenal of small talk strategies and mindsets and the reassuring awareness that we're all constantly a work in progress on this journey.

Small talk mastery isn't a pass/fail binary but a lifelong continuum of steadily sharpening our sensitivity to social subtleties. Like any skill, there will always be room for further refinement and new contexts to acclimate to. But by committing to the incremental improvement approach laid out here? You'll gain an advantage over the smoothest talkers by remaining humble, curious, and dedicated to the craft.

Who This Book Is For

So, who precisely is this book geared towards helping most? Well, the short answer is...pretty much everyone!

After all, struggles with small talk and related social anxiety are remarkably universal afflictions. You could be an extreme introvert, someone on the Autism spectrum, or just a socially overconfident person lacking self-awareness - chances are, you've been tripped up by casual conversation snafus before.

From college students feeling awkward at parties to newly single adults having to rediscover their mingling ability to career professionals realizing their networking incompetence has become a liability. An extensive range of experience levels and personal backgrounds can benefit from the self-awareness and skill development housed in these pages.

That said, if I had to zero in on the "prime" audiences, I'd highlight a few primary demographics:

- **Lifelong shy introverts and people who consider themselves socially awkward:** Those who've always lived more comfortably on the fringes of socializing mayhem but recognize we're missing out on connection opportunities that could enrich our lives.

- **Social anxiety sufferers:** No shame at all if clammy palms and panicky self-talk tend to accompany the mere thought of chit-chatting with fresh faces. This book is all about desensitizing those locked-up fears.

- **Ambitious career climbers:** Upwardly mobile young professionals inevitably realize shaky small talk skills can anchor their networking and people management progress at a certain point. This provides a friendly tune-up.

- **The perpetually curious and socially thoughtful:** For those eager to deepen their emotional intelligence and conversational range, this book contains wisdom for cultivating true social mastery over time.

So, whether you are preparing for a big occasion like a wedding, conference meet-and-greet, or new job or want to get more confident bringing casual charm to everyday life, there's something here for everyone. And hey, if you happen to be one of those frustratingly outgoing folks who are gabbing 24/7 without self-consciousness, this book can provide enlightening introspection on the receiving end of small talk.

Either way, I'd highly recommend clarifying your specific small talk struggles and pain points before we dive too deep together. That self-awareness will help you extract maximum value from this book and provide crucial context for tailoring the techniques uniquely to you. So, let's start getting those clearly defined right now.

I know we like to skip the question at the end of the chapter and move on to the next chapter right away. Unfortunately, doing so will keep the knowledge in your head without impacting your life. So, stop and complete this self-assessment before moving on to Chapter 1.

There will be an opportunity for reflection and practice at the end of each chapter. Don't skip those! Commit to completing all the practice steps before moving forward in the book. Do the work and change your life!

Self Assessment

RATE YOUR CONFIDENCE IN these various social situations on a scale of 1-10, with 10 being very confident and 1 being no confidence whatsoever:

- Meeting new people one-on-one

- Approaching a group of strangers

- Keeping a conversation flowing naturally

- Transitioning small talk to deeper topics

- Making small talk in professional settings

- Attending and making small talk at networking events

Go ahead and jot down your scores - we'll reference them periodically as you start bulking up those self-assurance muscles.

**Next, take an honest inventory of your current
minor talk abilities.**

- What communication skills do you already feel
  relatively confident in?

- Maybe you're an active, engaged listener who puts
  people at ease.

- Or someone who maintains warm, approachable
  body language and eye contact.

- Don't gaslight yourself out of identifying
  strengths.

- These are just a few examples. Yours may be different entirely.

**Get clear on your weakest small talk links for the
more challenging self-love test.**

- Are there nerves around initiating conversations
  from scratch with fresh faces?

- Falling into funks and zoning out during lulls?

- Knowing when to transition from light banter
  into deeper rapport territory?

- Or something else!

Most importantly, think about the specific small talk scenarios that routinely spike your anxiety or leave you flustered.

- Work functions?

- Dinner parties?

- Speed dating or any situation where you're rapidly meeting many new folks?

Jot down those flare-up contexts and triggers—they'll be mission-critical as we explore tactics for taming your unique anxieties and avoidance reflexes. As you identify and become aware of these issues, you can move forward knowing you can change.

Whatever YOUR profile of insecurities and weak spots happens to be, know you aren't alone; more importantly, this isn't permanent. You absolutely can and WILL befriend casual conversation through the holistic combination of reshaped mindsets and tangible tactics.

That's precisely why I want you to get those vulnerabilities explicitly spelled out in your raw language. Seeing those former flubs and limitations scribbled out will help us isolate precisely where to concentrate our combined efforts in the coming chapters.

More importantly, it'll be much more rewarding for you when we start transmuting each of those old fears and stumbles into rehabilitated STRENGTHS. Soon enough, you'll find yourself naturally slipping into conversation flow states where jumbled words and tense silences of your social past are distant memories. Instead, you'll tap into a deep reserve of confidence from the rock-solid skills and mindsets we build together.

Once you've finished this task, let's move on to Chapter 1 – The Challenges of Small Talk.

Chapter 1

The Challenges of Small Talk

(So, SERIOUSLY, IF YOU didn't complete the Self-Assessment at the end of the introduction, do that before starting this chapter. Thanks, you won't be sorry!)

My mother told me during my formative years that I could be anything I put my mind to, and I believed her. I never doubted my intellect, problem-solving skills, or business abilities. Where I struggled was meeting new people anywhere.

Our family lived in the same neighborhood until I graduated high school. The kids from our neighborhood and our church were lifelong friends, and almost all of us went to school together. With close-knit groups like this, there wasn't any need for making small talk with new friends, so it was a skill I never learned or saw modeled.

My first experience with a fear of rejection happened when I entered middle school. Kids were drawn from several elementary schools, so very few of my friends were in my classes. I was small for my age, so I felt awkward next to many kids who already looked like adults. And, let's face it, middle school kids can be so mean to those like me who don't know how to fit in.

My heart raced as I entered the classroom, my eyes darting around, looking for a friendly face or an empty seat that felt safe. Kids were already grouped into cliques, chatting and laughing effortlessly, while I stood on the fringes, feeling like an outsider. My small stature made me stand out, but not in the way I wanted. Instead of blending in, I felt like a glaringly obvious misfit.

In high school, the situation didn't improve. I was still smaller than most of my peers, and my petite frame made me look more like a sixth grader than a teenager. This physical difference compounded my social anxiety. I constantly felt the weight of my self-consciousness, as if everyone's eyes were on me, scrutinizing my every move and word. I was terrified of saying the wrong thing, of making a mistake that would invite ridicule and laughter from the more confident, dominant kids who seemed to rule the school.

I share this because many don't know where our social fears began. Some started at home, perhaps in an environment where open communication wasn't encouraged, or criticism was more common than praise. For others, like me, these fears took root in school. Schools, with their complex social hierarchies and relentless peer pressure, can be breeding grounds for anxiety and self-doubt.

Reflecting on my experiences, I realize how these early struggles shaped my social interactions for years. The fear of ridicule and rejection became deeply ingrained, making it hard for me to trust others and make friends. It wasn't until much later that I began to understand and address these fears, working to rebuild my confidence and learn how to connect with others genuinely.

Understanding the origins of our social anxieties can be a decisive step toward overcoming them. It allows us to see that these fears are often rooted in specific experiences and contexts rather than inherent to who we are. By acknowledging where these fears come from, we can begin to challenge and change the narratives that have held us back, paving the way for healthier and more fulfilling relationships.

My default coping strategies ranged from pathetically clinging to the few people I knew like a life raft to skulking around the outer edges doing my best "wallflower in important meetings" impersonation. Either way, I never felt confident enough to mingle and organize conversations organically.

But then I reached a point, personally and professionally, where avoiding small talk wasn't feasible. I had to find
ways to get comfortable putting myself out there, at least
on a surface level of chitchat. That meant addressing the
psychological demons that had been dictating my socially
anxious behavior for so long.

As I recounted, a lot stemmed from low self-esteem,
which convinced me I was inherently uninteresting or
unworthy of connecting platonically. Why would these
strangers want to engage with the real, flawed me? Keeping
people at a distance is much safer than never opening up.

That nasty inner monologue bred intense fears of rejection, which made me want to overcompensate by per-
forming this tiresomely calculated "perfect" persona during small talk attempts. Of course, all that overcompensa-
tion just backfired into coming across as inauthentic and
sweaty-palmed. A vicious cycle, if you will!

Understanding the Struggle

Let's be real here for a second—small talk can be brutally
challenging, even for those who don't identify as "shy"
people. And you know what? That's normal and okay
to admit! Engaging in casual conversation, especially with

folks you don't know well, is a nuanced social skill that nobody is born knowing how to master.

I mean, think about what we're asking of ourselves anytime we make small talk: put on a friendly but not overeager face, summon an arsenal of light subjects from our brains, speak loud enough to be heard without yelling, not to mention reading all sorts of subtle body language and social cues from total strangers. All while coming across as breezy, charismatic, and low-key amazing at this whole human interaction thing.

It's honestly an intricate dance we're doing, one that requires sharp cognitive skills and a fair amount of finesse. No wonder many of us get flustered or clam up when thrust into those situations! Expecting to be an instant small talk savant is like expecting someone to become a brilliant astrophysicist overnight – there's a whole skill set to develop first through practice and study.

Definition and Purpose of Small Talk

 So, what exactly is small talk? Picture it like this: small talk is the social equivalent of dipping your toes in the water before jumping into the pool. Those light, easy conversations help us warm up to each other. It's not about discussing the meaning of life or your deepest fears—save that for later. Small talk is like chatting about the weather, your favorite Netflix show, or the latest meme. The whole point is to make a connection, break the ice, and ease into more meaningful conversations. Think of it as the appetizer before the main course.

The primary purposes of small talk are building essential rapport, feeling each other out to see if there's a vibe worth exploring further, making people feel welcome and engaged, and establishing some short-term social parameters. This includes discussing the weather, commenting on your surroundings, or trading basic background info.

It's the shallow end of the conversation pool – nothing too splashy, just some gentle verbal wading to get a sense of who you're interacting with before deciding to swim further into the depths.

Common Misconceptions

Because small talk tends to be so deceptively tricky for many of us, it's inevitably spawned some silly misconceptions about what it should look like. Stuff like thinking you need to be a motor-mouthed comedian constantly cracking jokes and one-liners to be "good" at it.

There's also the bizarre belief that small talk means being fake, insincere, or putting on an over-the-top dialogue rather than just being your usual friendly self. There's also the trap of thinking that because it's called "small" talk, you need to keep interactions aggressively brief and surface-level to a fault.

Excellent small talk involves being relatively chill, adaptable, and modestly engaging. There is no need for comedy routines or faux personalities here. At its core, it's simply about creating temporary social comfort while gauging whether a person may be worth getting to know better over time. It's just a way to see who you want to know more, and the other folks are doing the same. It's a win-win.

Psychological Barrier

Social Anxiety and Shyness

Of course, plenty of psychological factors can disrupt the small talk process even when you understand its definition and purpose. Social anxiety is a major one, where you get hit with disproportionate feelings of fear, negativity, and self-consciousness when put on conversational display.

Imagine entering a room full of unfamiliar people who all seem to know each other already. Even if you're usually confident in different areas of your life, you might suddenly feel intensely shy and anxious in this setting. You become hyper-aware of every word you say and every move you make, as if you're under a microscope and everyone scrutinizes you: your heart races, your palms sweat, and your mind races with self-doubt.

That unsettling experience of wanting to be part of the social flow but feeling on the outside looking in? That's social anxiety rearing its ugly head, brutally short-circuiting your ability to make small talk without constant fear and awkwardness.

The Impact of Social Anxiety

Social anxiety doesn't just make small talk difficult; it can make even the most straightforward interactions feel daunting. The fear of judgment or rejection can be so overwhelming that it paralyzes you, making initiating or sustaining conversations hard. This can lead to a vicious cycle where the more you avoid social interactions, the more isolated you become, and the more your anxiety increases.

For instance, you might find yourself at a networking event, clutching your drink, trying to muster the courage to approach someone. The crowd's noise feels loud, and every laugh or glance in your direction seems loaded with judgment. You rehearse your opening line repeatedly in your head, but when the moment comes, you freeze or stumble, convinced you've made a fool of yourself. The anxiety becomes so consuming that you retreat to a corner, wishing you could disappear.

Overcoming Social Anxiety

Understanding the origins of your social anxiety is a crucial step towards overcoming it. Once you recognize that these fears are rooted in specific experiences and contexts, you can begin to challenge and change the narratives that have held you back.

Start by practicing small talk in low-stakes environments. Join a club or group where you share common interests with others. This can make it easier to initiate conversations, as you already have a built-in topic to discuss. As you become more comfortable, you can gradually extend these interactions to more challenging settings.

Mindfulness and cognitive-behavioral techniques can also help. Practice being present in the moment, focusing on the conversation rather than your internal anxieties. Challenge negative thoughts by questioning their validity and replacing them with more realistic, positive ones.

Seeking Professional Help

I want to be clear: self-help strategies aren't enough for everyone, and seeking a professional may be required for some. Therapists who specialize in social anxiety can provide you with tools and techniques to manage your stress more effectively. Cognitive-behavioral therapy (CBT) is highly effective in treating social anxiety by helping you change negative thought patterns and behaviors.

Medications can also be an option for some people, helping to reduce the intensity of anxiety symptoms. Discussing these options with a healthcare professional to determine the best approach for your situation is essential.

Social anxiety can be a formidable barrier to compelling small talk, but it's not insurmountable. By understanding its roots, practicing in safe environments, challenging negative thoughts, and seeking professional help, you can gradually build your confidence and improve your ability to engage in meaningful social interactions. Remember, the goal isn't to become the life of the party overnight but to take small, consistent steps toward feeling more comfortable and authentic in your social interactions.

Common Situational Challenges

But look, even if you've conquered those more considerable psychological roadblocks to a degree, plenty of super common situational factors still test our small talk skills. Let's examine some of the trickiest recurring scenarios.

Initiating the Conversation

This challenge NEVER seems to get any easier for me, no matter how often I face it. You've probably experienced it too: you're at a social or professional event, leaning against the wall, gathering the courage to join groups of people who seem profound in conversation as if they've known each other for years.

When exactly is the right moment to make your approach? Do you wait for a lull, a laugh, or just dive in? And how do you physically position yourself to slip into an existing conversation without feeling awkward? It's like trying to merge into traffic without any clear opening.

And then, once you've managed to join the group—gulp—you realize it's up to you to get the ball rolling. You can't just nod to whatever they discussed before you arrive; you must contribute something meaningful. Your mind races as you search for the perfect icebreaker. Do you comment on the event, make a lighthearted joke, or dive into a topic that might engage everyone?

It feels like walking through a maze of potential social blunders every time. Will they welcome your input, or will there be an awkward silence? Will you appear exciting and approachable, or inadvertently kill the conversation? These uncertainties can be paralyzing, making starting a conversation seem insurmountable.

Maintaining the Flow

For me, maintaining the flow of a conversation is often just as challenging as starting one. I'll get through the initial greeting or icebreaker question, feeling a moment of triumph as the first 30 seconds pass smoothly. But then... crickets. Suddenly, everyone's eyes are on me, and it's up to me to keep the conversation going with fresh comments and engaging questions.

Cue the mental blankness and conversational stall-outs. I find myself desperately trying to pull exciting topics out of thin air, my mind racing to come up with anything to avoid the awkward silence. Meanwhile, I'm also trying to read everyone's body language, searching for cues that might indicate if they're losing interest or if I'm potentially overstaying my welcome.

It's like juggling while riding a unicycle on a tightrope. I need to keep the conversation balanced, engaging, and inclusive while navigating the delicate dance of social interactions. One wrong move and the whole thing can come crashing down.

I constantly second-guess myself: Should I ask about their work or keep it light with a comment about the venue? Should I share a personal anecdote or ask for their opinion on a current event? And once I've exhausted a topic, how do I transition smoothly to the next without it feeling forced or unnatural?

In these moments, maintaining the flow feels like an intricate art form that I've yet to master. It requires a blend of quick thinking, genuine interest, and a touch of charisma—qualities that seem to come effortlessly to some but remain elusive to me. The pressure to keep the conversation lively and engaging is intense, and the fear of it faltering can be overwhelming.

Ending the Conversation

Eventually, every small talk interaction needs to end. Figuring out the precise moment to gracefully extricate yourself is a delicate dance. Stay too long after the conversation has run its course, and you risk becoming that conversational lingerer who can't take a hint, making everyone uncomfortable.

On the other hand, if you cut things off too abruptly, you might come across as disinterested or even rude. Mastering the art of the exit, with the perfect blend of politeness and firmness, requires real finesse and practice.

Recognizing the right moment to end the conversation is crucial. You need to be attuned to subtle cues—shifts in body language, waning enthusiasm, or repeated glances at the clock—that indicate that it's time to wrap things up. However, it's not just about identifying the right moment; it's also about executing the exit smoothly.

All these conversational stages are a gauntlet for those who haven't learned these skills. The excellent news is that this can all be learned!

External Factors

Cultural Differences

While respectful basic small talk tenets are relatively universal, different cultures bring unique nuances. An acceptable degree of personal space, volume, or directness varies. Some backgrounds may prioritize making direct eye contact as a sign of engagement, while others see it as disrespectful.

Not accounting for those subtle differences can inadvertently send the wrong social signals, hampering small talk before it starts.

Environmental Factors

Small talk is more challenging in some contexts than others based on environmental factors like noise, lighting, seating arrangements, or overall vibe. Engaging at a loud concert versus a cozy happy hour requires radically different approaches.

We went out for brunch with a couple of friends this past weekend, and just when we finished ordering, a musician started playing, accompanying a Flamenco dancer's performance. No more conversation was possible until that ended, so we all watched, clapped, and started chatting again.

Not getting tripped up by those variables and being able to adapt your conversation style and on the fly is a stealth aspect of small talk that doesn't get enough credit.

Generational Differences

I'm sure we've all noticed how different age groups tend to gravitate toward distinct small-talk vibes, too. A recent college grad who grew up with social media may gravitate toward a more ironic, meme-culture bantering style. Baby boomers communicate in a way that emphasizes direct, personal interaction and detailed, formal communication. While they have adapted to digital communication tools, their usage often reflects a preference for clarity and thoroughness. Understanding these characteristics can help bridge generational communication gaps and foster better interactions across age groups.

Real-Life Examples and Scenarios

Phew, I know - that's a lot of potential pitfalls to watch out for already, right? Now imagine layering all those anxiety sources, psychological traps, and contextual nuances on top of each other in the real world. It's no wonder so many of us get concerned in common small-talk scenarios like:

- Work happy hours – Navigating the jungle of coworker chitchat, where you must remain convivial yet professional. Not to mention accounting for subtle office politics regarding who gets conversational priority.

- Weddings—You must make the rounds, introducing yourself to clusters of strangers who are all bonded by knowing the couple is getting married, leaving you as the inevitable outsider.

- Networking events—These are places where everyone is there expressly to try and make new connections through small talk, ramping up the social pressures and judgments to a fever pitch.

- First dates are situations already dripping with potential romantic tension and overthinking, with the added sprinkles of having to find common conversation threads from scratch.

Any occasion where you're being asked to mingle and socialize outside of your familiar circles is pretty much a small-talk hot zone. Depending on the mix of circumstances and personal quirks involved, it's almost inevitable that most of us are going to struggle in at least a couple of areas of the process.

The Impact of Technology

Digital Communication

Of course, in today's age, we've got a whole new layer of small-talk stumbling blocks thanks to our collective reliance on digital communication. Quick - when was the last time you had an extended phone call that didn't involve just breezing through some perfunctory chit-chat to address practical logistics?

For many of us, the sheer act of holding a spontaneous casual conversation has become wildly unfamiliar compared to the asynchronous comforts of texting, emailing, and direct messaging. We've gotten rusty, is what I'm saying. And a lack of vocal practice only amplifies the challenges of small talk's in-person nuances.

Social Media

For example, look no further than the curated faux personas we cultivate over social media. When written words are your primary interaction channel, it's easy to meticulously construct this idealized "personal brand" of wit and cleverness. Gut instinct reactions get replaced with heavy self-editing.

This creates a weird dissonance when you have to drop the pristine cyber veneer and produce spontaneous casual conversation on the fly—something we've gotten progressively worse at as a society. Paradoxically, social media has made many of us worse at being, y'know ... socially functional.

When you're used to perfectly sculpting your persona and dialogue for public consumption, the rawness and real-time reactive flow of proper small talk can feel downright jarring.

I could probably spend another few thousand words recounting personal mortifying small talk or psychological studies on the phenomenon. But you get the idea by now, right? Navigating idle chit-chat smoothly requires a robust mental toolkit of skills many of us have yet to develop fully.

Identifying Personal Challenges

We've covered a lot of ground already regarding the psychological barriers and situational nuances that can disrupt our small talk abilities. But of course, those universal struggles tend to manifest in highly personal ways for each of us as individuals. That's why it's so important to ruthlessly identify your unique small-talk Achilles heels.

What specific inner demons or social scenarios have a way of throwing your mojo most severely out of whack? The more granular and self-aware you can get about your personal shortcomings, the better equipped you'll be to start dismantling them point by point.

For some, the root issue may be profound social insecurity that keeps them from ever feeling comfortable enough to attempt to put themselves out there conversationally. For others, the biggest struggle might be a tendency to overshare or dominate discussions without realizing it. Maybe your kryptonite is simply blanking on engaging topics to discuss and getting mired in awkward silence.

Whatever your small talk vices and vulnerabilities, it's crucial to outline them and define them. That's the first step towards facing them head-on without flinching through the mindset shifts and concrete strategies we'll explore throughout this book's later chapters.

Setting Goals for Improvement

After those honest self-assessments, the next logical step is to ponder where exactly you want to see growth and level up from your current small talk baseline. In other words, what are your personal goals for harnessing your social evolution?

Your goals will probably be like the challenges just discussed in this chapter. My first goal was simply to face my fear by attending one event each week that I would have avoided otherwise. A reasonable goal might simply be to initiate three brief small-talk exchanges over the course of a day. Whatever challenge you can face right now, that's a good goal at this point.

The key here is to be specific yet forgiving with the goals you set for yourself. Don't simultaneously aim for a full Jedi-level mastery of witty banter and social grace. That's like deciding you want to lose 50 pounds and be able to run a marathon by next month - setting yourself up for intense pressure and likely burnout.

Instead, work on incremental, moderately stretched targets that steadily build your small talk skills and confidence over time. Not only are those small milestones way more attainable, but each one you hit provides a gratifying sense of momentum to propel you toward whatever larger social mastery you aspire to.

Be sure to document these aims clearly, too. Writing out objectives with some sort of specificity, like "I want to increase the number of new people I can confidently approach from 2 to 5 during the next office party," adds definition and conviction. It transforms abstract desires into actionable missions you can fully wrap your head around achieving.

Overcoming the Hurdles

I'll be the first to admit that as simple as goalsetting may sound, it's often one of the trickier parts of the overarching small-talk improvement process for so many of us. Our nagging self-doubts and insecurities can crowd out any constructive thoughts about what positive changes we want to manifest.

- "Who am I trying to kid? There's no point in setting social goals when I will just mess it all up anyway."

- "Even if I wanted to be good at small talk, I

don't have the right kind of personality ever to get there."

- "My fear of rejection will never disappear, so why try forcing something unnatural?"

We've all been there with the toxic mind funks, #amirite? Those incessant streams of self-sabotaging blather make it brutally tempting to surrender and accept our perceived small talk futility as a regrettable personality flaw to work around.

Well, I'm here to tell you that those types of destructive thought patterns are exactly what we need to start dismantling if you ever want to break through to new levels of social comfort and confidence. They're the micro-instincts of shutting down and self-marginalization that we need to override through focused mindset shifts and commitment to actionable progress.

Mindset Shifts

You've heard the adage that perception is reality, right? When it comes to our temperament and self-beliefs around conversational skills, that tendency towards self-fulfilling prophecies is crazy apparent. Tell yourself you're doomed to be the world's most awkward wallflower, and ... guess what? You'll absolutely start nailing that wallflower act consistently. Change your language, change your life!

That's why one of the most crucial parts of small talk improvement must start between the ears—identifying the unhealthy or self-limiting mindsets that have been our default settings for too long and replacing them with more optimistic, opportunity-oriented perspectives.

An easy one to start with? Actively working to reframe small talk not as this big overwhelming skillset to master all at once but rather a collection of micro-competencies to practice piecemeal at your own pace. Breaking it way down like that can instantly ease a lot of the performance anxiety that so often derails us.

From there, it's about chipping away at your unique small talk sore spots using a potent blend of mindset modifications and specific new behaviors to rehearse in lower-stakes scenarios. This is highly personal, gradual work that takes persistence and self-compassion.

For instance, maybe you constantly fall into the trap of negative self-talk about being "just one of those quiet, socially awkward people." To disrupt that, you could start inserting simple mantras throughout your day, celebrating small conversational wins, no matter how micro.

- "I asked the barista how her day was going - go

me!"

- "I said hi to the neighbor walking her dog and asked the dog's name."

We're adults now, and it's time to put away those fears and insecurities from our childhood. Part of that is rejecting those words others say about us that we now say to ourselves. Start listening to that inner voice and determine whether it's true or not, whether it's productive for your life or not.

If it's not true and productive for you, then just say, Stop, that's not true. Then tell the correct, true statement. And do that until your inner voice is only speaking the truth. (A book you may want to read on this subject is "The Big Leap" by Gaye Hendricks. This book changed my life because you don't see these things until you see them!)

Over time, shifting from a fixed mindset of ineptitude to highlighting your slow but steady improvement can profoundly shift your confidence levels and how others perceive your demeanor. It's powerful stuff! Change your inner talks, change your life!

Building Confidence

In many ways, increased confidence is the inevitable byproduct of successfully shifting your mindset away from overly self-critical and pessimistic default settings. As those old reflexes ease up and you start stacking conversational micro-wins, a positive feedback loop starts taking shape.

You feel slightly more self-assured heading into the next interaction attempt, so you bring a smidge more easygoing energy and openness. That causes things to flow incrementally better than usual, further validating your belief in steady improvement. Lather, rinse, incremental progress loop!

Of course, confidence is a finicky beast to harness when it comes to small talk. It's not just about global self-assurance but also situation-specific poise. You may feel like a social butterfly at work or family functions, yet getting thrown into an event filled with strangers might trigger all the old anxieties and ugly feelings.

That's exactly why having modest, micro-level aims rather than shooting for mythical, instant smooth-talker status is so powerful. Hit those bite-sized, hyper-specific goals enough times, and your mobility between different comfort zones and contexts starts expanding rapidly.

Then one day, seemingly out of nowhere, you'll find yourself dropping into a high-pressure small talk situation that would've once crippled your nerves...and feeling preternaturally calm and capable. Oh, yeah, this is just another scenery change to flex those chat skills I've been working on.

It's vital not to sleep on the accumulating confidence dividends of those small wins. They're not something to dismiss as incremental baby steps. Rather, they're the only sustainable path to building up that deep reserve of unshakable savoir-faire that people universally admire.

Incremental Progress

This brings me to a crucial point that I think bears repeating as clearly and emphatically as possible: improving at small talk is a PROCESS, not something to be rushed or attempted in gigantic desperation heaves. It's a journey of small, low-stakes practice modules and mental adjustments that gradually compound into profound, naturalized growth over time.

We're talking about dismantling habits and behavioral patterns around socializing that have likely been ingrained over decades. Those sedimentary layers of knee-jerk responses simply don't melt away because you read an awesome book about conversation skills (although congrats on being awesome enough to buy this one!).

So, suppose you're willing to embrace a mindset of incremental progress, where you feel good about baby step after step rather than berate yourself for not shape-shifting into Ryan Gosling overnight. In that case, that's already a massive hurdle cleared. It's all about moving the needle in small doses at whatever comfortable pace works for you as an individual.

The only prerequisite for success on this path is dogged consistency - a willingness to keep lacing up those small talk shoes daily and incrementally leaning into the skills that prime you for more seamless banter down the road.

It's committing to inserting casual transitional small talk reps into the most mundane daily interactions possible. Chatting up with the grocery store checkout person about the weather. Smiling and exchanging neighborhood updates with my elderly neighbor while grabbing the mail. Playfully bantering with cashiers about them having any interesting plans for the upcoming weekend.

At first, I'm sure those fleeting exchanges sounded robotic and really cringey to outsiders observing. But the more micro-reps I worked in, the more my muscle memory for natural conversation flow started getting encoded. Slowly but oh-so-surely, easygoing chit-chat stopped feeling like this precarious balancing act I had to tiptoe through.

That's the power of embracing small talk as an incremental process of desensitization and small improvements - stuff that used to trigger hair-raising terror could eventually start feeling as low-stakes and casual as brushing your teeth. No need to put insane pressure on yourself to level up to Chris Rock comedy specials right away! Focus on building up those baseline smoothness reserves through modest daily actions, and one day you'll wake up cleared for the conversational penthouse suite.

Self-Reflection and Assessment

WRITE DOWN YOUR THOUGHTS on the importance of small talk. List any misconceptions you have about it.

- Think about any preconceived notions or beliefs you have about small talk. Do you see it as pointless or superficial? Do you think it's only for extroverts?

- Write down these misconceptions and consider where they might come from. Have past experiences shaped these beliefs? Have you heard others express similar views?

Reflect on your experiences with social anxiety, fear of rejection, or low self-esteem. How have these affected your small talk?

- Think about times when you felt socially anxious or feared rejection. How did these feelings affect your ability to engage in small talk?

- Write about specific situations where these feelings either hindered or helped your small talk efforts.

- Consider how low self-esteem has impacted your confidence in starting or maintaining conversations.

Recall a situation where you struggled to start, maintain, or end a conversation. Describe what made it challenging.

- **Starting the Conversation:** Can you remember a situation where you struggled to start a conversation? What made it difficult for you to initiate?

- **Maintaining the Conversation:** Think of a time when you found it hard to keep a conversation going. What challenges did you face in maintaining the flow?

- **Ending the Conversation:** Reflect on an instance where you felt awkward ending a conversation. What made it challenging, and how did you handle it?

Think of a time when cultural, environmental, or generational factors influenced your small talk. Write about how you handled it.

- **Cultural Factors:** Have you ever had a conversation where cultural differences played a role? How did you navigate these differences to keep the conversation flowing?

- **Environmental Factors:** Consider a time when the setting influenced your small talk, such as a noisy party or a formal event. How did you adapt to the environment?

- **Generational Factors:** Recall a situation where age differences influenced the conversation. Did you find it challenging to relate, and how did you bridge the generational gap?

Reflect on how digital communication and social media have impacted your face-to-face small talk skills.

- **Digital vs. Face-to-Face:** How has your online communication differed from in-person interactions? Do you find it easier or harder to make small talk face-to-face after frequent use of digital communication?

- **Social Media Influence:** How has social media shaped your expectations or approach to small talk? Do you feel more connected or disconnected from others in face-to-face interactions as a result?

- **Online Habits:** Reflect on your texting, messaging, or social media habits. Have these habits impacted your ability to engage in spontaneous conversations in person? If so, how?

- **Adapting Skills:** Have you noticed any skills from online communication that have helped or hindered your face-to-face small talk? How have you adapted your approach to small talk in the digital age?

Identify your specific challenges with small talk.

To sum up my own small talk Kryptonite - starting conversations from scratch, under-confidence causing me to fade into the wallflower role, struggling to adapt my energy/formality level for the specific situation at hand, and falling into over-edited/rehearsed patterns from too much digital posturing. An area I still need to work on. Not overthinking the need for clean conversation exit strategies and exacerbating every instance of a chat winding down organically.

Write down three specific goals for improvement.

- **Goal Setting:** Consider areas where you want to improve your small talk skills. These could be related to starting, maintaining, or ending conversations gracefully.

- **Specific Goals:** Write down three specific, achievable goals. For example, "Initiate a conversation with a new person at each social event I attend," "Practice active listening to keep conversations flowing," or "Learn and use five new conversation starters."

- **Action Plan:** Briefly outline how you plan to achieve each goal. What steps will you need to take to improve these areas? How will you measure your progress?

With those top focus areas identified and you have reflected on your specific sticky points, I'd say we've got a solid game plan for what comes next.

Listen, I know that was a lot of psychological espresso to sip—examining all the potential emotional potholes, social dynamics, and contextual snafus that can brutally undermine our small talk abilities. Enough cold-water perspiration for one chapter. Let's dive into Chapter 2, where we'll learn the Basics of Small talk!

Chapter 2

The Basics of Small Talk

HAVE YOU EVER FELT your stomach do flips just thinking about talking to strangers? Yeah, me too. I've been there, blending into the wallpaper at social events like it was my job. But don't worry; I've got some tips to help you go from awkward silence to small talk pro.

I bet you can relate. Picture me gripping a lukewarm cup of coffee like it's a lifeline while everyone else is out there chatting away like it's no big deal. Sound familiar? Well, hang tight, because we're about to dive back into that memory and pull out some profound wisdom.

Starting Conversations Smoothly

You know that moment when your brain decides to take an impromptu vacation right as you need to start talking? Yeah, I've been there and done that. (I've got the T-shirt to show you.) I stood silently for a full minute, trying desperately to conjure up something—anything—to say to the person next to me at a networking event. Pro tip: Staring blankly rarely breaks the ice effectively.

Effective Icebreakers

Alright, let's talk about why breaking the ice is actually worth the effort. I get it—hugging the outskirts of a group feels safe and waiting for someone (preferably no one) to approach you seems like the better option. But let's be real, that's not going to do much for your career, your growing business, or building those deeper friendships we all crave.

So, what works? I'm so glad you asked. Here are some go-to conversation starters that have yet to let me down:

1. Compliment something specific about their appearance and dig into the story behind it.

2. For example, "I love your scarf! The pattern is gorgeous. What's the story behind it?"

3. Show genuine interest in a topic they're already chatting about.

4. Comment positively about the food or drinks, then ask about their experience.

5. Play the newbie card and ask for their expert ad-

vice.

6. Something like, "I'm new around here. Any recommendations for good coffee shops?"

7. Mention a recent event or speaker and get their
take on it.

Remember, the goal here isn't to blow them away with
your wit; it's just to open the door for more conversation.
Think of it as a gentle knock instead of a full-on charm
offensive.

Creating Positive First Impressions

First impressions are a lot like book covers—they might
not tell the whole story, but they sure do influence whether
someone wants to keep reading. And believe me, I've had
more than my fair share of "book cover" mishaps.

Let me paint you a little picture: There I was, trying to
ooze professionalism when suddenly, my elbow decided
to go rogue. In what felt like slow motion, I watched as
my water glass tipped over, unleashing a mini tsunami
across the once-pristine tablecloth. Ice cubes scattered like
they were in a race, and water dripped steadily onto my
brand-new suit pants.

In that split second, I was convinced my shot at making a good impression had evaporated faster than spilled water on a summer sidewalk. But here's the thing: it's not about being flawless. It's about rolling with the punches when things go sideways. So, I took a deep breath, looked at the stunned faces around me, and said, "Well, I guess I really know how to break the ice!" The tension popped like a balloon and, before I knew it, everyone was laughing.

That little moment of vulnerability? It ended up creating a connection long after the water dried. It turns out that people value authenticity way more than perfection. Sometimes it's as easy as admitting you're nervous, like, "I was so jittery about this event that I almost wore mismatched shoes!" Who knew?

The writers of the screenplay "Miss Congeniality" understood this. Actress Sandra Bullock played a tough FBI detective who had to go undercover in a beauty pageant to catch a terrorist. Of course, she was transformed from a mannish appearance to a gorgeous beauty queen on the outside, but she was still the same person on the inside.

The movie's main character, Gracie Hart, is surrounded by beautiful women competing in this pageant. While Gracie is transformed into an equally beautiful woman, her genuine small talk, which she learns throughout the film, makes her popular with the other contestants. This is a great film to watch and make notes from, so I strongly suggest you do so.

So how do you create a positive first impression? Here's my tried-and-true playbook:

1. Flash those pearly whites genuinely. A warm smile acts like a beacon of friendliness.

2. Make eye contact but avoid staring contests. We're aiming for connection, not creepy vibes.

3. Use their name but double-check that you heard it correctly first. Calling someone "Bob" when they're "Rob" rarely ends well.

4. Listen actively and show genuine interest. We'll explore this further later but remember: Use two ears and one mouth proportionally.

5. Be yourself because authenticity magnetizes people. Don't pretend to be someone you're not - it's exhausting, and folks usually see right through it.

I'll never forget when I stood in front of my bathroom mirror, practicing my introduction for a networking event. I must've said, "Hi, I'm Judy Best, and I'm a real estate entrepreneur," at least fifty times, trying out different tones and even throwing in some hand gestures. Just when

I thought I had it down, my cat strolled in, gave me that classic "you're talking to yourself again, human" look, and walked off like I was the crazy one.

But hey, that practice totally paid off. When I got to the event, my introduction flowed out effortlessly, and I actually felt pretty confident approaching people. I just had to keep reminding myself to smile and make good eye contact. My handshake has always been firm, but if yours isn't, it's worth practicing that, too.

My name is straightforward, but people still manage to mix it up, calling me Julie or something else entirely. I just smile and say, "Nope, I'm Judy, but you can call me whatever you want." That usually does the trick.

Here's the thing: everyone you meet is probably just as nervous as you are. If you focus on making them feel at ease, you'll be amazed at how quickly your own nerves start to melt away.

Choosing Safe Topics

So, we've nailed the first impression, the ice is officially broken, and now comes the big question: What on earth do we talk about? This is the moment when visions of awkward silences loom large, like a conversational desert stretching endlessly ahead. But don't worry—I've got you covered. Here's a little secret: The best small talk topics often hide in plain sight—sometimes, quite literally, right under your nose.

Safe and Engaging Topics

Imagine this: You're at a gallery opening, surrounded by abstract art that looks suspiciously like a toddler's finger-painting session gone off the rails. You're doing your best to appear thoughtful and cultured, nodding at a canvas that could either be a sunset or the aftermath of a pizza explosion. Sound familiar?

This exact scenario happened to me not too long ago. I clutched a glass of so-so wine, staring blankly at a perplexing piece. My brain was scrambling for something clever to say when the woman beside me leaned over and whispered,

"I can't decide if it's a sunset or a pizza explosion. What do you think?"

And just like that, the ice was obliterated. We spent the next hour laughing and coming up with all sorts of wild interpretations of the art around us. It was a great reminder that sometimes the best conversation starters are there, waiting for us to notice them. Just ensure you're not chatting up the artist before trying that one!

Looking for some go-to conversation starters? Here's a quick, chatty list that's served me well over the years:

1. **Comment on the venue or event:** "What do you think of the decor?" or "Been here before?"

2. **Light current events:** Stick to movies, books, or tech. "Seen the new Marvel movie yet?"

3. **Travel talk:** "Have you been anywhere cool recently?" or "What's your dream destination?"

4. **Hobbies:** "What do you enjoy doing in your free time?" You might uncover a secret passion!

5. **Food and drink:** Chat about the event's menu or ask for local restaurant tips.

6. **Weather:** Yep, it's a classic. Just try to spice it up a bit!

7. **Local tips:** New in town? Ask for recommendations—people love playing tour guide.

8. **Pets:** Always a winner but get ready for a flood of
cute pics.

9. **Music:** "How's the playlist?" Just be ready for
some surprising tastes!

10. **Career chat:** "How'd you get into your field?"
People usually love sharing their work stories.

There you have it—a treasure trove of conversation
starters sure to keep the chat flowing. Whether you're talking about the latest movie or bonding over a mutual love
for travel, these topics will help you easily navigate any
social situation. Just remember, the key is to be genuinely
interested and let the conversation unfold naturally. Before
you know it, you'll make connections and leave a lasting
impression without breaking a sweat.

Topics to Avoid

On the flip side, steer clear of diving headfirst into polariz-
ing politics, grim medical stories, heavy trauma tales, heat-
ed debates on current events, or anything that's likely to
bring down the vibe. These topics can sink rapport faster

than a lead balloon, making everyone tense or awkward. Save the deep stuff for when you've built a solid foundation of trust with lighter, more upbeat conversations.

Trust me, I learned this the hard way at a barbecue when I naively thought discussing a controversial news topic would spark some lively conversation. By the time the burgers were flipped, half the guests were glaring at the other half, and I was mentally mapping out the quickest escape route. Lesson learned!

Lesson learned! Here's a quick rundown of topics you'll want to steer clear of, especially when you're just getting to know someone:

1. **Politics:** Unless you're at a political event, keeping this one off the table is best. No one's ever had their mind changed over appetizers.

2. **Religion:** Much like politics, it's a deeply personal and potentially divisive subject. Save the deep existential stuff for a philosophy club meeting.

3. **Money:** Talking about salaries, costs, or financial status can make people squirm. If you're a banker, you may get away with it.

4. At our favorite jeweler's open house a few years

ago, the salespeople met the couples at the door to adorn the women in jewels. Our banker arrived right after us, admired the necklace around my neck, and handed my husband his business card, saying, "Call me tomorrow. That looks lovely on your wife's neck." LOL. It was a fun event where chatting was easy, and the banker handed out all his business cards!

5. **Health issues:** Unless they bring it up first, keep your gallbladder stories to yourself—especially over guacamole.

6. **Age:** Asking someone's age, particularly women, can be a major faux pas. In some cultures, it's a no-go, and you might end up with a drink in your face.

7. **Appearance:** Comments about weight, height, or any physical attributes are a minefield. Instead of saying, "Have you lost weight?" try, "You look fantastic! What's your secret?"

8. **Relationship status:** Questions like "Why are you still single?" or "When are you having kids?" should be banished from your small talk arsenal.

9. When you meet a couple who are obviously together, it's always fun to ask, "How did you two meet?" (And, if you are asked that, make sure you keep that story brief!)

10. **Controversial news:** Stick to the fluffier side of current events. A cute story about a panda at the zoo beats diving into the latest political scandal any day.

11. **Gossip:** Talking smack about others, especially mutual acquaintances, is a major no-no. It only makes people wonder what you're saying about them behind their backs. Instead, stick to safe topics like weekend plans or hobbies.

12. **Overly personal questions:** Respect boundaries and avoid prying into private matters. Questions like "How much do you earn?" or "Why did your last relationship end?" are not small talk material.

Keep it light and fun, and you'll navigate any social situation like a pro!

So there you have it—a guide to dodging conversational landmines and keeping the vibe upbeat. Mastering the art of small talk isn't about being perfect; it's about knowing what to steer clear of and how to keep things light and engaging. With these tips in your back pocket, you're ready to tackle any social situation, from casual coffee chats to networking events, without breaking a sweat.

Remember, the goal is to build connections and enjoy the conversation. By focusing on positive, inclusive topics, you'll not only make others feel comfortable but also create an atmosphere where real rapport can flourish. So next time you find yourself mingling, just relax, be yourself, and let the conversation flow naturally—you've got this!

Building Blocks

It's not just about asking the right questions—it's about sharing a bit of yourself, too. Nobody enjoys feeling like they're in the hot seat of a one-sided Q&A. The trick is to toss in your own thoughts and stories, then swing the focus back to your conversation partner.

Questions, Comments, and Listening

Think of a good conversation like a game of catch—toss out a question, share a comment, and listen actively as the conversation bounces back and forth.

For example, at a recent backyard BBQ, my new neighbor Jenny started telling me about her puppy's latest shoe-chewing escapades. Instead of grilling her about dog training techniques, I laughed and said, "Oh, I've been there—my couch cushions barely survived the teething phase! But who can stay mad at those puppy-dog eyes?" That little story earned me some cuddle time with her furry troublemaker.

Balancing curiosity about others with your own stories makes for a conversation that flows naturally and feels like a friendly chat.

Creating a Natural Flow

Keeping a conversation flowing smoothly is like being the DJ at a party—you need to know when to switch tracks and when to let the beat ride. It's all about keeping the vibe just right.

I remember when I first tried to get better at small talk. I'd walk into a conversation with a mental checklist of questions, and then I'd robotically tick them off, one by one. "How's the weather? Check. What do you do for work? Check. Have you seen any good movies lately? Check." The result? Conversations that felt stiff and awkward, like I was reading from a script. I'm pretty sure people thought they were chatting with an overly curious robot.

The game-changer for me was realizing that great conversation isn't about sticking to a script—it's about being in the moment and letting things unfold naturally. It's kind of like jazz—you have a rough idea of where you're going, but the magic happens when you go with the flow.

First, don't be afraid to follow the thread of an interesting topic. If someone mentions they love cooking, don't just nod politely and move on to your next question. Jump in! Ask about their favorite recipes, share a story about your own kitchen disasters, and let the conversation take on a life of its own. The best chats happen when you go off-script and explore new territory together.

Next, consider transitional phrases like "That reminds me of..." or "Speaking of..." as your conversational secret weapons. They help you glide from one topic to the next without those awkward grinding gears, making everything feel seamless and natural.

Sharing your experiences adds depth and invites others to do the same. It's all about balance, though—remember, it's a dialogue, not a monologue. If they mention they love hiking, you might say, "I'm into hiking too! There's nothing like the views from the top." Then toss the ball back with, "What's your favorite trail?"

Don't fear a little silence, either. A brief pause gives both of you a moment to gather your thoughts. It's not the end of the world; it can be refreshing. Don't let it linger too long, or you'll wonder if you've got spinach in your teeth.

And finally, read the room. Pay attention to their body language and tone. If they start looking around like they're planning their escape, it's probably time to switch topics or gracefully wrap things up.

With these tips in your back pocket, you're not just ending a conversation but setting the stage for the next great one.

Reflections & Practice

LET'S REINFORCE THE DEVELOPMENT of smooth "basics" and secure small talk success in the future! Try these exercises tailoring baseline skills:

1. Craft 10 Friendly Icebreaker Greetings

• Write down 10 different greetings that you can use to start a conversation. These should be friendly and engaging.

• Examples: "Hi, I'm [Your Name]. How's your day going?" or "Hey, have you seen the latest [movie/show/news]? What did you think of it?"

• Try to vary them based on casual settings, professional events, or meeting new classmates.

2. Brainstorm Safe Topics Suiting Various Contexts

• Make a list of generally safe and appropriate topics for different settings. Consider what would suit casual gatherings, professional environments, and more formal events.

• Examples: "What's your favorite way to spend a weekend?" for casual settings or "Have you been working on any interesting projects lately?" for professional environments.

• Consider topics likely to be of mutual interest and avoid controversial subjects.

3. Roleplay Introduction Exchanges with Trusted Friends

• Find a friend or family member willing to help you practice your small talk skills. (You can also practice in front of a mirror, but friends or family are a better choice.)

• Roleplay different scenarios where you practice introducing yourself and starting a conversation.

• After each roleplay, ask for feedback on what went well and what could be improved. Focus on areas like your tone, body language, and the flow of the conversation.

• Try to practice in various settings to build confidence and adaptability.

By practicing these exercises, you will develop a solid foundation in small talk, find areas for improvement, and set actionable goals to enhance your social interactions.

Now that we've built fundamental competence kicking off and sustaining basic conversations, it's time to unlock the real game changers that elevate exchanges from mundane niceties into memorable mutual understanding.

Next, we're diving deep into high-level listening techniques and verbal and non-verbal skills that demonstrate true engagement, empathy, and emotional intelligence conversing. Instead of biding time through routine small talk, I'll teach you how to make people feel genuinely valued, understood, and fascinated during conversations. Soon you'll practically see minds and hearts opening as souls connect across unlikely common ground through the power of your non-judgmental presence.

Let's dive into Chapter 3 – Listening and Engagement!

Chapter 3

Listening and Engagement

PICTURE THIS: YOU'RE AT a networking event, surrounded by a sea of unfamiliar faces. Conversations swirl around you like a chaotic breeze, laughter echoes in the air, and you suddenly feel like you're the odd one out. Sound familiar? Been there, done that—more times than I can count. As an introvert thrown into the deep end of business networking, I quickly learned that small talk isn't just about filling the silence—it's about truly listening and engaging with the people around you.

Active Listening

Let me take you back to my early days of networking, when I'd cling to the crowd's edges, phone in hand, hoping no one would notice me. Spoiler alert: That strategy worked about as well as trying to catch water with a sieve. It didn't take long to realize that I had to ditch my digital security blanket and engage if I wanted to make real connections. Active listening isn't just hearing someone out—it's about really focusing on what they're saying and showing that you're present in the conversation.

Techniques to Show Genuine Interest

One night, fate had a sense of humor and cornered me with an eager entrepreneur at a chamber of commerce mixer. My first instinct? Plot an escape. But instead, I decided to lean in and practice some active listening. I kept steady eye contact, nodded in all the right places, and really honed in on his words. Before I knew it, I was genuinely interested in his story about starting a family landscaping business. Not only did I learn something new, but I also made a meaningful connection—all because I chose to listen with intention.

All this talk about active listening might sound like common sense, but trust me, it's easy to forget when you're in the thick of a conversation. So, how do you show interest without turning into a robot reciting techniques? Here's the lowdown:

First off, **eye contact** is vital—but don't overdo it and turn it into a staring contest. Keep it natural. Pair that with a few non-verbal cues like nodding or leaning in slightly, and you're already on the right track.

Now, this next part can be tough: **Resist the urge to interrupt or jump in with your own story.** I get it—sometimes someone says something that sparks a thought, and you're dying to share it. But hold back. Let them finish before you dive in. People hate being cut off, and nothing kills the vibe faster.

Instead, when it's your turn, **ask a follow-up question** that shows you're really paying attention. For example, when my friend was talking about their new job, I didn't just nod along mindlessly. I asked, "How's the new work environment treating you?" It was a small thing, but it showed I was genuinely interested.

Another solid move? **Paraphrase what they've said** to make sure you've got it right. When my cousin was raving about her trip to Paris, I'd say things like, "So you hit the Eiffel Tower on day one?" It's a simple way to show you're engaged and want to hear more.

And don't wait for high-stakes situations to practice this stuff. Try it out in everyday chats with friends or family. They're the perfect test subjects, and it'll help you nail your small talk game when it really counts.

Demonstrating Engagement

Engagement isn't just about listening—it's about jumping into the conversation with both feet. My usual bench-sitting approach had its moments, but I knew I needed to step it up.

At one particularly nerve-wracking event, I decided to push myself out of my comfort zone. Instead of hanging back and hoping someone would come talk to me, I spotted a small group chatting about local restaurants and thought, "Why not?" I took a deep breath and wandered over. When the moment was right, I casually mentioned a new sushi spot I'd tried downtown. Suddenly, I was in the middle of a lively discussion about hidden culinary gems in the city—right in my wheelhouse.

Here's what I've learned about really showing you're engaged:

- **Share your own experiences that fit the conversation.**

- **Ask follow-up questions that keep the chat going.**

- **Give genuine compliments or show appreciation for what others share.**

- **Use people's names occasionally—but don't overdo it.**

- **Show enthusiasm with your tone and expressions.**

For example, at a team meeting, I made a point to summarize what others had said before chiming in with my thoughts: "So, Sarah, you think we should move the deadline to Friday to keep the quality up? I'm with you on that because..." It showed I was listening and helped build on the conversation in a way that valued everyone's input.

Body Language

Now, let's talk about the conversation happening without words. Body language can speak louder than anything you actually say. I used to be the person who'd practically blend into the wallpaper at events, but I've been working on stepping up my non-verbal game, and it's made all the difference.

Using Non-Verbal Cues

Remember when I talked about the power of a simple smile? It's amazing how something so small can break down walls and make you seem approachable. But smiling is just the start—your whole body tells a story.

At a recent conference, I watched a friend of mine in action. Her posture was open, her shoulders back, and she used her hands to emphasize her points. You could practically feel the energy and warmth radiating from her, and people naturally gravitated towards her. So, I decided to give it a try, and wow, did it change how people responded to me.

If you want to up your non-verbal game, try practicing in front of a mirror. Here's what works for me:

- **Keep an open posture:** No crossed arms or hunched shoulders.

- **Lean in slightly:** It shows you're interested and engaged.

- **Mirror the other person's body language:** Don't overdo it.

- **Use hand gestures:** They can really emphasize your points.

- **Keep your facial expression relaxed and engaged:** It goes a long way.

You know those little kids you see on social media striking poses and saying affirmations in the mirror? There's something to that. If runway models practice their walk, why shouldn't we practice our networking stance? The more we work on it, the more natural it becomes.

I used to dread making calls to strangers so much that I'd find any excuse to put it off. But I knew it was crucial for my career, so I decided to try something different. I'd strike the Wonder Woman pose before picking up the phone. Yep, I'd stand up, feet shoulder-width apart, hands on hips, shoulders back, chest out, head high—the whole superhero stance.

At first, I felt ridiculous. But you know what? It worked. It reminded me that I could tackle tough tasks and overcome my fears. Over time, that pose didn't just change my body language—it changed my mindset. Each time I did it, I felt stronger, more capable, and ready to take on whatever challenge was in front of me. Now, whenever I'm faced with something daunting, I tap into that feeling of empowerment, knowing I've got the tools to succ

Eye Contact and Facial Expressions

Let's be real—making eye contact can feel super awkward, especially for us introverts. But it's key to showing you're engaged and building trust. I used to struggle with it because it felt like I was under a spotlight. And when it gets uncomfortable, the instinct is to look away, right? Been there, done that.

Here's a little trick that helped me: instead of staring straight into someone's eyes, try focusing on their forehead or lips. It'll still seem like you're making solid eye contact but without the pressure. As you get more comfortable, you'll start to enjoy it because you'll pick up on the emotions behind their words—excitement, fear, you name it. Their eyes tell the story.

Facial expressions are like seasoning in a conversation. A raised eyebrow? That's curiosity. A slight frown? Concern. A warm smile? Pure appreciation. Let your face naturally react—it makes you come across as more engaged and approachable.

Practical Tips for Eye Contact and Facial Expressions:

1. **Aim for 60-70% eye contact during conversations.** It's easier in a group because you can glance around at others, which takes the pressure off.

2. **Shift your focus** between the forehead, eyes, and

lips—just do it subtly. Need proof? Ask a friend to look at your forehead and lips while you tell a short story. Looks like good eye contact, right?

3. **Let your facial expressions flow naturally** with the conversation. I'll admit, I struggle with this too. When I "try" to look sympathetic or encouraging, it can backfire. Case in point: at our wedding, my husband, despite being sick, insisted on singing to me. I tried encouraging him with my expression, but he just shook his head like, "Please stop!" So, I ditched the forced expression and just smiled with tears in my eyes, and that did the trick.

4. **Practice in front of a mirror** (I know, I know—but trust me on this). Watch how your face reacts when you're actively listening. Not too shabby, right? You can tweak it as needed, but I bet you're better at this than you think.

5. **Remember to blink!** Seriously, natural blinking is a must. This isn't a staring contest—active listening is about being focused, not creepy. You're paying attention because what they say matters, not because you're trying to win a no-blinking challenge.

Mastering eye contact and facial expressions might feel like a lot at first, but with some practice, it'll become second nature. The key is to start small—try these tips in casual conversations, and before you know it, you'll be a pro at making genuine connections.

Remember, the goal here isn't to be perfect; it's to be present. The more comfortable you get with these techniques, the more natural they'll feel, and the easier it will be to truly engage with others. So, next time you're in a conversation, relax, let your eyes and expressions do some of the talking, and watch how much more connected you'll feel with the people around you.

Ultimately, it's all about making others feel heard and valued. Whether you're sharing a laugh, offering support, or just chatting about the weather, your body language can make all the difference. So go ahead, put these tips into practice, and see how they can elevate your conversations from good to great.

The Tone of Voice and Pace

How we deliver our words can make all the difference in how they're received. As someone who's navigated my fair share of awkward social situations, I get it—some of us talk fast and quietly, trying to get through the discomfort as quickly as possible. Others might be loud and speedy, eager to share their stories. But here's the thing: when you're racing through your words or cranking up the volume, it can be tough for listeners to really catch what you're saying.

Learning to play with your tone and pace is like finding your groove. Think of it as setting the perfect vibe for a conversation. You don't want to leave people straining to hear you or wondering what they missed because you sped through your point. It's all about hitting that sweet spot where your voice is clear, your pace is just right, and your message lands perfectly.

Here's a fun way to practice, turn up the TV or radio at home and start telling a story. Record yourself at different noise levels, adjusting your volume and pace each time. It might feel a little weird at first, but you'll find the rhythm that works with practice. Before you know it, you'll speak at a level and speed that's easy to follow, even in noisy settings.

I had my own lightbulb moment at a public speaking workshop. The instructor stressed the importance of changing your tone and pace to keep people engaged. So, I decided to test it out during my next networking event. When I shared my elevator pitch, I slowed down, played with my tone, and emphasized the key points. Suddenly, people were leaning in, asking more questions, genuinely interested in what I was saying. It wasn't that my business had magically become more exciting—I just got better at telling the story.

Pro Tips for Nailing Your Tone and Pace:

Start by speaking clearly and steadily—no need to rush. Use pauses like a pro to highlight important bits and give your listeners a moment to soak it all in. And don't be afraid to switch up your volume here and there to make key points stand out. Matching your tone to the emotion behind your words helps your message hit home. Oh, and if you're up for a challenge, try practicing with tongue twisters. Not only will it make your speech clearer, but it's also entertaining!

So next time you share your story, remember, it's not just about what you say, but how you say it. Find your rhythm, have fun with it, and watch your words come to life.

Responding Thoughtfully

Active listening isn't just about soaking up information—it's about how you respond, too. In my early networking days, I'd either freeze up or blurt out whatever random thought popped into my head. Spoiler alert: neither of those approaches led to great conversations.

Here's the thing: when you're truly listening, it's not about rushing to come up with your reply. If you're just waiting for your turn to talk, you've already stopped listening. It's like putting yourself ahead of the person you're supposed to connect with. But when you focus on really understanding what they're saying, the conversation naturally flows, and you'll often find yourself asking follow-up questions instead of scrambling for a response. It's a game-changer, especially since it means you are becoming more comfortable on the networking scene.

How to Give Meaningful and Natural Responses

I've had my fair share of awkward moments while practicing my networking skills, but one thing that helped me find my groove was volunteering to be a door greeter at events. I'd say the same things over and over: "Hi! So glad you're here. Check in at the table before heading to the buffet—doesn't the lunch smell amazing? Two Sisters Cafe is catering today!"

It might sound repetitive, but those interactions were pure gold. People would greet me by name after reading my nametag, and when they'd join me at the table later, they'd always mention that I'd greeted them at the door. It made follow-up conversations super easy because we'd already broken the ice.

That became my go-to approach once I realized how much easier relaxing and having fun with it was. Now, I aim to keep things relaxed and natural—no pressure, just a good, effortless flow.

Let's switch back to active listening for a moment. If you are actively listening, even during introductions, it's easy to respond well. Folks love to talk about themselves. Since they love to tell their stories, you can easily express your interest in that story by asking for more details.

So, you've navigated the conversation and actively listened, and now it's time to respond in a way that really connects. Here's how to keep the conversation flowing smoothly while making it enjoyable for both you and the person you're talking to:

1. **Relax and Breathe:** Seriously, take a moment to slow down. Deep breaths help you stay present and truly listen to what's being said.

2. **Reflect and Respond:** Echo back something they've shared to show you're tuned in. Something like, "Wow, I never thought about entrepreneurship at such a young age. What got you started?"

3. **Keep the Curiosity Going:** Ask follow-up questions to dive deeper. It shows you're genuinely interested, and let's be honest, who doesn't love talking about themselves a little more?

4. **Share but Keep It Short:** If you've got a relevant experience, share it—but keep it brief. Then, toss the ball back to them with another question, like, "I went through something similar when... How did that change your goals?"

5. **Compliment Sincerely:** A genuine compliment
   or word of encouragement goes a long way. But
   remember, only say it if you mean it—people
   can spot fake flattery a mile away. If their passion
   inspired you, let them know. It's a great way to
   connect on a deeper level.

In the end, conversations are about connection, not
just exchanging words. By responding thoughtfully and
focusing on understanding the other person, you're not
just making small talk—you're building relationships that
matter. So go ahead, relax, listen, and let your responses
flow naturally. You've got this!

Reflections & Practice

NOW THAT WE'VE COVERED key aspects of listening and engagement, it's time to put these skills into practice. Remember, like any skill, these techniques improve with repetition. Don't feel discouraged if it feels awkward initially—even most seasoned networkers started somewhere!

Pair up with friends and practice active listening. Take notes on how it felt and what you noticed.

Find willing friends or family members to help you practice. Take turns sharing a story or experience for about 5 minutes each. While one is speaking, the other should focus on active listening techniques. Pay attention to your body language, facial expressions, and quality responses.

After each round, discuss what you noticed. How did it feel to be a listener? Did you find your mind wandering at any point? When you were a speaker - did you feel heard and understood? This exercise can be eye-opening and help identify areas for improvement.

Observe people's body language in a public setting. Note positive and negative cues.

Next time you're in a public place—café, park, or even a grocery store waiting line —observe people around you. Look for examples of positive body language: open postures, engaged facial expressions, and mirroring between-person conversation. Also, note negative cues: crossed arms, lack of eye contact, and turned-away body positions.

This exercise will help you become more attuned to non-verbal communication and how it impacts interactions. You might be surprised how much you can "read" without hearing a word!

Practice responding thoughtfully to common small talk questions. Please write down your responses and evaluate them.

Take time to brainstorm common small talk questions you might encounter at networking events or social gatherings, such as "What do you do?" "How's your week been?" or "What brings you to this event?" Then, practice crafting thoughtful, engaging responses.

Please write down your responses and evaluate them. Are they open-ended, inviting further conversation? Do they offer a bit of personal information while still being professional? Are they authentic who you are?

Here's an example:

Question: "What do you do?"

Poor response: "I'm in marketing."

Better response: "I run a digital marketing agency that helps small businesses grow their online presence. I love seeing local entrepreneurs succeed. What's your experience been with marketing your business?"

This response answers questions, shows enthusiasm for your work, and opens the door to further conversation.

As we conclude this chapter on listening and engagement, I hope you're beginning to see how these skills can transform your small talk from awkward encounters to meaningful connections. Remember, it's not about being the loudest voice room or having the most exciting stories. Often, it's about being present, showing genuine interest, and responding thoughtfully.

My journey from an introvert who felt uncomfortable at networking events to someone who can confidently engage in small talk has been transformative. Mastering these skills has been crucial, though only sometimes easy. I still experience moments of self-doubt, but with practice and patience, I've seen a dramatic improvement in my interactions and connections.

As you continue honing your listening and engagement skills, you'll discover that small talk becomes less of a chore and more of an opportunity to learn, connect, and grow personally and professionally.

In our next chapter, we'll build on these foundational skills and explore how to ask the right questions—another crucial aspect of mastering the art of small talk. After all, knowing how to listen and engage is only half the battle. Knowing what and how to ask can elevate your conversational skills to new heights. So, are you ready to become a question master?

Let's plunge into an exciting world of inquiry in Chapter 4 – Asking the Right Questions.

Chapter 4

Asking the Right Questions

ONE OF THE TRICKIEST parts of small talk is keeping the conversation alive. But here's the secret sauce: asking open-ended questions. Master this skill, and you'll be able to transform surface-level chit-chat into deeper, more meaningful conversations that build real understanding and connection.

In this chapter, I'll spill the beans on some insider techniques for crafting intriguing questions that are guaranteed to get people talking. Keep these gems in your back pocket, ready to spark meaningful dialogue in both personal and professional settings.

Open-Ended Questions: Your Conversation Superpower

Imagine yourself in a cozy coffee shop—baristas chatting with regulars about their latest adventures, friends laughing and catching up, and even strangers striking up animated discussions in line. What's their secret? You guessed it: skillfully crafted open-ended questions.

Unlike those basic yes/no questions that can stop a conversation in its tracks, open-ended questions invite people to openly share their stories, opinions, and experiences. They create space for a real exchange—where you can discover common ground and take the conversation to new depths.

Having a few go-to questions can be a game-changer. Here are some of my favorites that never fail to get the conversation flowing:

- **How did you start your current career or hobby?**

- **What's the most interesting thing you've learned lately?**

- **What's a goal or dream you're working toward right now?**

- **How do you stay motivated and inspired in your daily life?**

- **How do you balance your personal and professional life?**

These thoughtful questions show that you're genuinely interested in people's stories—their journeys, dreams, and the experiences that have shaped them. When you ask questions like these, you're not just making small talk—you're forging connections, celebrating what makes each of us unique, and setting the stage for deeper conversations.

But here's the thing: even the best questions can flop if you don't deliver them with care. Timing is everything—so make sure you're tuned into the conversation's rhythm. Ask with genuine curiosity, not just to fill a silence. Remember, your goal is to build trust and connection, not to check off boxes in a social checklist.

And don't forget—it's not just about asking questions—it's about how you listen and respond. A well-placed question followed by active, empathetic listening can open the door to memorable and impactful conversations. So, as you dive into your next chat, think of your questions as keys to unlocking deeper connections—ask them with sincerity, listen with your heart, and watch how your conversations transform.

Follow-Up Questions

Starting a conversation is one thing, but keeping it flowing? That's where the magic happens, and it all comes down to follow-up questions. This is the secret sauce that transforms a simple chat into something deeper and more meaningful.

But let's be honest—there's a fine line between being curious and turning into an overly enthusiastic detective. You don't want to pepper someone with a rapid-fire Q&A session that feels more like an interrogation than a conversation. The goal is to balance letting the conversation breathe and diving into the good stuff.

I want to share a personal story here. When I started a new job in a new community where I knew no one, I felt pretty lost. But on my first day, two smiling gals, Tammie and Tracey, stepped into my office and invited me to join them for lunch. At the restaurant, they asked me lots of questions, genuinely wanting to get to know me. In return, I asked them about their careers and personal lives. From that first meeting, a trio of best friends was born. We've shared every celebration and tough situation since, and it all started with a simple give and take. We found enough common ground to stick together without being just alike.

Here's what I've found: trust your gut. After really listening to what someone's saying, follow your curiosity. Maybe their career path has taken some unexpected turns, or perhaps they've faced challenges that have shaped who they are today. These are the moments where you can dig a little deeper—where you might find a shared experience, like I did with Tammie and Tracey, or discover that their story sounds much like your own.

The key here is to listen for relatable threads and explore them gently. It's not about grilling someone for details but about creating a space where they feel safe to share. Sometimes, the best way to encourage that openness is to offer a bit of your own story first. When you're willing to share, it invites others to do the same.

We all naturally desire to bond over shared experiences, but it happens best when we feel safe to open up gradually. So, create that space—ask thoughtful, compassionate follow-up questions that show you're more interested in understanding the person than dissecting their life choices. This approach not only keeps the conversation going but also builds the kind of connection that sticks.

Keeping the Conversation Going

Keeping a conversation flowing smoothly is like dancing with a partner—you want to move in sync, responding to each other's steps without missing a beat. One of the best ways to do this is by asking thoughtful follow-up questions. The magic happens when you pick up on the details people share, turning those into natural stepping stones for the conversation to continue.

For example, when a new client, Ella, shared how she pivoted from nursing to holistic health coaching after an injury, I didn't just nod and move on. Instead, I gently asked about her recovery journey. That simple follow-up led to a deeper conversation about the alternative therapies that transformed her career and life. It wasn't just about getting more information; it was about keeping the conversation flowing naturally, without abrupt changes in direction.

Good follow-up questions don't interrupt the rhythm—they keep it going, allowing the conversation to unfold organically. They're inspired by the nuances people drop in their answers, like finding a new path to explore together. Here's how I might do it:

- **"Wow, that sounds like quite an adventure!**

What surprised you most about that experience?"

- **"Could you tell me more about that holistic health concept you mentioned?"**

- **"How did you handle the challenges of such a big career shift?"**

The goal isn't to force the conversation into a specific direction but to let it evolve naturally. By paying close attention and using small verbal clues as launch points, you create a conversational flow that feels effortless, almost like a well-rehearsed dance.

Follow-up questions also allow you to clarify anything you didn't quite understand. I love to say, "That sounds fascinating—could you explain it a bit more?" It's a way to keep the conversation moving forward while showing that you're genuinely interested in what they're saying.

Remember, this isn't about grilling someone for details. It's about engaging in a dance of dialogue, where questions and responses flow smoothly into the next. When you let your curiosity guide you, the conversation becomes less about extracting information and more about sharing a moment of genuine connection. The result? A seamless, enjoyable exchange that leaves both parties feeling heard and understood.

Balancing Questions and Comments

As your small talk mentor, I want to highlight a crucial skill today: striking the right balance between asking engaging questions and sharing your own insights. Too many rapid-fire questions can feel intrusive, while over-sharing can dominate the conversation and leave the other person feeling sidelined. The sweet spot lies in a natural give-and-take flow that keeps the conversation balanced and engaging for both parties.

Strategically Blend Asking and Offering

We've all been there: you start with a great open-ended question about someone's recent career change, but after a flurry of follow-up questions, you notice they're looking a bit overwhelmed. Suddenly, the conversation feels one-sided.

Here's the trick: after one or two dynamic questions, pivot to sharing a short, relatable insight from your own experience, then smoothly guide the conversation back to them. Think of it as a conversational dance—moving gracefully between listening and sharing.

For example, you might say: "Wow, Danielle, directing your first full-length film at only 19 sounds intense! What inspired you to take on such an ambitious project so young?" After she shares, you could respond with, "I love your passion for elevating marginalized stories. It reminds me of when I published my first book to amplify unheard voices. Did you have any surprising lessons from your project?"

By briefly sharing your own milestone, you show that you're genuinely listening and that you can relate, setting the stage for an uplifting, mutual exchange.

Mindfully Avoid Hogging the Spotlight

It's easy to get caught up in our own excitement and end up monologuing about our achievements. But to keep the conversation balanced, it's important to pass the mic. I learned this the hard way when I excitedly shared every detail of my recent promotion, only to realize later that my friend hadn't even had a chance to share her equally exciting news.

To avoid this, keep your turns concise—aim for about 30 seconds when sharing your updates. Use the rest of the time to engage through questions that show you're interested in their story, too. Remember, a great conversation is a two-way street.

Read Verbal and Non-Verbal Cues

Finally, be attentive to the other person's verbal and non-verbal cues. If they're energetically recounting their latest adventure, dive in with enthusiastic questions. But if they seem hesitant or fidgety, it might be your turn to take the lead in the conversation or shift the topic to something lighter.

By listening closely and observing body language, you can adjust your pacing and approach, ensuring the conversation flows naturally and leaves both of you feeling connected and understood.

Mastering the art of conversation isn't about memorizing techniques or following a strict formula—it's about finding that sweet spot where both you and the person you're talking to feel heard, valued, and engaged. When you balance asking with offering, curiosity with sharing, and listening with responding, you create a space where real connections can grow.

Think of a conversation like a well-tended garden. It requires the right balance of attention and care—sometimes, you need to plant new ideas, and other times, you water the ones that have already been shared. You pull a few weeds by gently steering away from awkward moments to allow new thoughts to bloom. With a little patience and the right touch, you'll cultivate conversations that are both vibrant and meaningful, leaving both of you eager to see what blossoms next.

So next time you find yourself in a conversation, remember it's not just about what you say but how you nurture the exchange. Lead with genuine curiosity, share enough to keep things interesting, and always be mindful of the cues that help guide the flow. With practice, you'll find your conversations flourishing, creating connections that last long after the words have been spoken.

Reflections & Practice

DEVELOPING SKILLS IN ASKING the right questions and maintaining conversational balance takes time and effort. Here are some exercises to help you hone these abilities.

Write ten open-ended questions you can use to encourage detailed responses.

Flex creative questioning capacities by brainstorming ten open-ended icebreakers that spark intrigue and flowing responses. Consider what thought-provoking questions might energize these folks:

- Your passionate novelist friend outlines their tales

- A public health professional sharing insightful trend

- Fellow volunteers relishing making local parks equitable

- An eco-tour guide revealing stunning nature mysteries

1. "What originally made you love writing fantasy fiction, Grace?"

2. "How do you stay motivated persevering long nights in the E.R., Russ?"

3. "What surprised you most witnessing how climate shifts impacted polar bear habitats?"

Soon, these cues turn second nature, chatting up strangers at events, too!

Practice asking follow-up questions based on initial responses. Roleplay with a partner.

Finding willing friends to roleplay back-and-forth "question and response" rounds helps immensely with modeling smooth follow-up forms. One partner asks the starter query, listens fully to the response, and then artfully crafts an additional question that digs deeper into details within their answer.

Such practice instills reactive rapport-building by leveraging what information is naturally uncovered in the existing flow rather than following rigid scripts. Keep exchanges conversational!

For example:

You: "What originally inspired you to become a sign language interpreter, Pamela?"

Them: "Growing up with a deaf cousin who struggled with being excluded from family conversations. I hated seeing that happen..."

You: "I can imagine witnessing barriers to inclusion so young felt frustrating. Are there advocacy issues improving accessibility and representation you feel passionate about currently?"

Engage in a conversation where you balance questions and statements to maintain a natural flow.

Final Words

Don't just stay on the sidelines—jump in! Start balancing your curiosity with thoughtful sharing by striking up conversations with baristas, fellow travelers, or friendly neighbors. These everyday interactions are your practice ground, where you can hone your skills and find your conversational rhythm.

After each conversation, take a moment to reflect. Did you ask too many questions? Did you share too much without giving the other person space? Use these reflections as stepping stones to fine-tune your approach for the next conversation, finding that sweet spot where connection truly happens.

Remember, the goal isn't perfection—it's progress. Every conversation is a chance to learn, to grow, and to build your confidence. Mastering the art of asking the right questions isn't just about small talk; it's about forging meaningful connections and creating engaging conversations that leave a lasting impact.

Whether you're navigating the professional networking scene, making new friends, or strengthening bonds with your team, these skills are your secret weapon. They open doors to deeper relationships and richer experiences.

As we move forward, we'll tackle the challenge of overcoming anxiety in social situations. Putting yourself out there can feel intimidating, even when you're armed with great questions. But don't worry—Chapter 5 is all about building confidence and managing those nerves. Get ready to conquer your networking jitters and step into small talk with confidence and ease. The next chapter is your gateway to becoming a conversation pro!

Chapter 5

Overcoming Small Talk Anxiety

FOR MANY OF US, small talk can feel like walking on a razor's edge, trying to stay balanced while dodging the awkward silences that follow the obligatory weather chat. Maybe you've been there, cringing at the memory of a joke that landed with a thud at a networking event. If you're nodding along, trust me, you're in good company—even the most outgoing folks sometimes stumble through social interactions.

Back in the day, I used to dread small talk like it was some social obstacle course. I'd watch in awe as those smooth talkers glided from one lively chat to the next while I was left feeling like I was floundering in the deep end, no matter how much I rehearsed in my head. The effort to keep a conversation going drained me more than any public speaking gig ever could.

But here's the thing: nobody becomes a small talk pro overnight. It's a skill, and all skills require practice. The more I pushed myself through those sticky situations, the more I realized that an awkward pause or a joke that didn't land wasn't the end of the world. In fact, every one of those cringe-worthy moments added to my social toolbox, making the next conversation a little less daunting.

This chapter is packed with down-to-earth tips to help you develop a more authentic presence, roll with the punches, and, most importantly, show yourself some grace in casual social settings. With these tools, what once felt like a dreaded chore will become surprisingly enjoyable. So, let's dive in and build the confidence you need to make small talk feel as easy as chatting with an old friend.

Building a Foundation of Confidence

Confidence can be a game-changer when it comes to making small talk feel less like a chore and more like a chat with a friend. For me, it's all about keeping a few key things in mind. First off, I remind myself that my self-worth isn't hanging by a thread during any single conversation. Even the smoothest talkers have their awkward moments—trust me, they've been there, too. Instead of sweating it, I've learned to laugh it off and see every little slip-up as a chance to get better. After all, nobody's grading these conversations, right?

I also try to focus more on listening than on crafting the perfect response or silently judging myself. Most people love to feel heard and showing genuine interest with a few follow-up questions can make things flow a lot easier. When the conversation starts feeling like a one-person show, or I sense an awkward pause creeping in, I've found that asking open-ended questions about their latest trip, their adorable pets, or their work can bring things back to life. It's amazing how much smoother things go when you're just trying to connect rather than impress.

And let's talk about mindfulness—because, yes, it actually helps! When I start feeling those nerves creeping up, a few deep breaths can do wonders to calm the mind and keep me grounded in the moment. Staying focused on the person in front of me helps me dodge the overthinking trap. Plus, the more I let go of the need to be perfect and just enjoy the conversation, the more confident (and dare I say, charismatic) I become.

Boosting Self-Assurance

Changing the thought patterns that fuel our social jitters has been a game-changer for me. Here are some mindset techniques I use to keep my cool:

- **Catch and Replace Negative Thoughts.** You know those sneaky thoughts like, "I'm too awkward" or "I have no idea what to say." When they pop up, I consciously replace them with something more positive like, "I'll give this a shot" or "I can handle whatever comes my way." It's amazing how much lighter you feel when you stop letting those thoughts take control.

- **Recall Your Wins and Redefine Success.** I boost my confidence by remembering past social wins, like making a new friend laugh or leading a great conversation. Success doesn't mean being perfect; it's about enjoying the moment and making real connections. I let go of trying to be a conversation superstar and focus on having fun instead.

- **Have a Few Go-To Topics and Actively Listen.** I keep a mental list of easy topics, like the latest game or a popular show, to pull out if the conversation stalls. But more importantly, I focus on listening and responding with genuine interest. Asking follow-up questions not only keeps the chat going but also shows I care about what the other person is saying.

- **Embrace Pauses and Use Positive Body Language.** Not every conversation needs to be a fast-paced exchange. Letting a silence happen naturally gives everyone a moment to think. Paired with positive body language—like smiling and maintaining eye contact—these pauses can deepen the connection.

- **Lighten Up with Humor and Start Small.** A little humor can go a long way in easing tension. If I stumble over my words, I'll chuckle and say, "Guess my brain hasn't had its coffee yet!" Starting with low-stakes interactions, like chatting with the barista, also helps build my social confidence before diving into bigger social situations.

- **Remember Everyone Struggles Sometimes.** Even the most outgoing people have their off days. Most folks are too busy thinking about themselves to judge us harshly. And when a conversation doesn't go perfectly, I remind myself that it's all part of learning. Each success, no matter how small, makes the next conversation easier.

As we build confidence through these strategies, it's important to remember that staying present and calm during conversations plays a huge role in feeling at ease. That's where mindfulness comes in.

Practicing Presence with Mindfulness

Staying present when chatting with others is critical to connecting. It's easy to space out or start overthinking. Mindfulness helps quiet my racing thoughts so I can focus on the person speaking. This focus makes dialogue smoother and more enjoyable for both of us. Here are some tips for using mindfulness to stay tuned in:

- **Breathing and Grounding:** Taking two to three deep, slow breaths when I feel my mind racing brings physiological calm. Inhaling deeply into the belly, feeling it expand and slowly exhaling helps relax a tense body. I consciously do this before attending networking events. These breaths remind my body that I am safe and have a plan that works. Every time your mind starts these fear tactics, these breaths will reset your mindset that there is nothing to fear.

- **Observing Thoughts and Emotions:** If I catch thoughts like "I don't have anything interesting to add" or "they seem bored," I acknowledge and then release them. Getting wrapped up in self-criticism makes me withdraw. By nonjudgmentally observing and then letting such unhelpful narratives pass by, I prevent descending into an anxiety spiral. Sometimes, this happens when the conversation shifts to more technical talk. Since I'm not a techie, I can't contribute much to those subjects. My husband, who owns a technology company, loves being drawn into those conversations. I've learned to handle this by laughing and saying, "You're over my head. I'll leave you guys to talk. Nice to meet you." Then, I wander off to find someone I have more in common. This way, I gracefully exit the conversation and move on to more relatable discussions. Sometimes, moving on is the best idea!

- **Active Engagement:** Sometimes, I immediately relate to what the other person is saying. When I become impatient to share my experiences or begin to prepare a response, I must reflect inwardly, "Just listen for now." Sinking into receiving rather than transmitting mode allows fuller understanding. For example, another real estate investor shared their recent acquisition and redevelopment of a multi-family property. This long, interesting story prompted several memories of similar properties that I wanted to share, but staying in active listening mode allowed me to keep the focus on the speaker. This show of interest ultimately enriched our exchange and growing relationship, where we grew from our shared experiences.

- **Embracing Silence and Reflection:** Rather than nervously jumping in during natural lulls, I take pauses as opportunities for both of us to gather our thoughts or transition between weighty topics. Sitting calmly through these gaps conveys that stillness holds meaning and that filling quiet moments with noise is unnecessary. For example, a few ladies and I met weekly for a Mastermind meeting. When it was my turn in the hot seat, I shared a recent struggle, and the others offered their ideas, thoughts, and questions about my situation. Instead of immediately responding, sitting in silence for a few minutes allowed me to seriously consider their input, giving each suggestion the weight it deserved.

The next time you catch your mind drifting as someone shares with you, gently shift your focus to the gift before you—another living being entrusting you with their thoughts and energy. This remembering helps steady wandering attention toward what matters most.

Techniques to Move Conversations Forward

With mindfulness, patience, and a bit of humor, silence can transform from a conversation killer into a thoughtful, blossoming space where something beautiful is budding between two minds. Practicing some responses I'll show you shortly will defuse tension, silently communicating, "This break feels natural to me, too." Each time you bravely stay open during gaps without recoiling, you build self-trust in your dialogue skills. Here are some examples of ways to handle lulls gracefully without panicking:

- **Come Prepared with Topics:** Entertainment and pop culture are easy conversational springboards. For example, ask, "Have you read any good books lately?" This question can easily lead to a discussion about shared interests or recommendations.

- **Ask Open-Ended Questions:** Ask lots of open-ended questions and encourage longer responses to keep the conversation flowing. For example, "What do you enjoy doing on weekends?" invites the other person to share more about their interests and activities.

- **Follow Up on Their Responses:** Keep the conversation moving by asking related questions. For instance, if they say, "I enjoy dining out and fine wines," you can respond, "Me, too! Where have you had the most interesting meals recently?"

- **Make Observational Comments:** Spark new topics by pointing out things in your environment. For example, "They're playing great music here tonight!" can lead to a discussion about music preferences or memories associated with certain songs.

- **Give Affirmations and Reassurance with Positive Feedback:** Simple affirmations like "Great point!" or "I never thought of it that way" show that you value their input.

- **Summarize Key Points:** You demonstrate that you've been listening by summarizing key things they've shared. Doing so shows that you are engaged and paying attention.

- **Share a Relevant Anecdote:** Reciprocate sharing by telling a relevant story of your own. For example, "That reminds me of a funny story..." helps build a connection through shared experiences.

- **Address Long Pauses Light-heartedly:** For instance, "Now that we've solved all the world's problems, what's new with you?" can lighten the mood and steer the conversation in a new direction.

- **Have an "Out" Ready:** Sometimes, you may need to politely exit the conversation. For instance, "It was great chatting! I'll have to tell my friend about that movie. Enjoy the rest of your day!" leaves the interaction on a positive note. Or, "Can I have a second business card? As I'm networking, I'd love to give a card to someone you need to meet." This way, they're happy to send you on your way!

Small talk might seem like a daunting mountain to climb, but with the right tools and mindset, it becomes less of an uphill battle and more of a pleasant stroll. We've walked through strategies for building confidence, staying present with mindfulness, and moving conversations forward—all designed to help you feel more at ease in any social setting.

Remember, no one becomes a conversationalist overnight. It's a journey, and every interaction is an opportunity to practice and grow. Whether you're chatting with a barista or navigating a networking event, these moments are chances to refine your skills and build meaningful connections.

As you put these techniques into practice, be gentle with yourself. There will be awkward pauses, missed cues, and the occasional foot-in-mouth moment—but that's all part of the process. Each stumble is a step forward, making the next conversation a little easier and more enjoyable.

The beauty of small talk is that it opens doors. It's the gateway to deeper relationships, opportunities, and shared experiences. So, as you step out into the world with these new strategies in hand, embrace the imperfections and celebrate the progress you're making. With time and practice, what once felt like a dreaded chore will transform into an effortless, engaging dance of words.

And remember, even the best dancers stumble now and then—what matters is that you keep moving and connecting. You've got this!

Reflections & Practice

STRENGTHENING SOCIAL SKILLS AND confidence takes gentleness, patience, and practice. Be encouraged that even the liveliest conversationalists once felt awkward when young or entering unfamiliar gatherings. It simply took repetitively pushing past discomfort to develop abilities that now appear effortless.

1. List strategies that help you feel more confident in social settings.

One of the best ways to build social confidence is to reflect on your past social successes. Another powerful technique is affirming your positive qualities. Identify your strengths, such as your sense of humor, emotional intelligence, or ability to listen attentively.

Preparation can also ease social anxiety. When stuck, a mental list of starter topics, such as favorite books, TV shows, hobbies, or recent events, can provide potential opening topics.

If you need more ideas, review this chapter for more confidence-building strategies.

2. Practice mindfulness techniques before a conversation to stay present

Here are a few to get your practice started:

- Pause to breathe - Take a few deep, mindful breaths before chatting to ground nerves so you stay present.

- Repeat calming phrases - Whisper positive mantras like "I am open. I am confident" to redirect racing thoughts.

- Notice sounds around you - Listen to ambient sounds in your environment to distract your inner critic with sensory details.

- Observe thoughts nonjudgmentally - Witness anxious self-talk, then practice releasing those thoughts to prevent spiraling.

- Visualize talking openly - Picture yourself laughing and connecting in exchanges you anticipate manifesting positive experiences.

- Scan for body tension - Check shoulders, jaw, fists, and stomach for tightness. Proactively relax areas carrying stress.

- Focus on wishing silent goodwill for the person speaking — Wishing well to those around you silently is a good practice, even as you live daily. I push out positive thoughts and prayers for people as they walk by or enter my spaces throughout my day.

3. Create a list of strategies to handle awkward silences.

I've shared my best tips in this chapter, so pick out the ones that work best for you. Start with eye contact and a smile, and remember to ask open-ended questions.

Let me know if any examples need more clarification or detail! I aimed to reframe the tips as direct second-person guidance.

We've covered core skills for approaching small talk with less anxiety and more confidence. Nice work! With mindful presence and the ability to roll with pauses, chatty activities can now seem delightful instead of dreadful.

Where do we go from here? Shake off any lingering unease and give your newfound talents a good-natured pat on the back. Then brace yourself for fresh social playgrounds.

It's time we up our game, meeting more complex situations head-on with wisdom and wit. What if parties felt exciting instead of exhausting? What if business mixers were full of fascinating people rather than forced phoniness? What if family gatherings deepened understanding across generations?

The next chapter will discuss making great first impressions, handling conflict gracefully across different personalities, and forging bonds with nearly anyone through compassion. Are you ready? Splendid, off we venture together to Chapter 6 – Adapting Small Talk to Different Solutions.

Chapter 6

Adapting Small Talk to Different Situations

I PAUSED IN MY neighbor's driveway, the sound of laughter and music spilling out from her lively house party inside. My palms grew clammy around the pineapple upside-down cake I'd baked, and I could feel my heart racing as I took in the scene—cars packed the street, and strangers mingled with ease just beyond the door. Anxiety tightened its grip, whispering that I should turn back and retreat to the comfort of my quiet home.

But I knew growth didn't happen by sticking to what's comfortable. I'd been making strides in feeling more at ease with casual conversation, and now was the time to put that progress to the test. My husband, ever the extrovert, gave my arm a reassuring tug. "You'll be fine. You'll have fun!" he said with a grin.

"You've got this," I told myself, taking a few steadying breaths. With the cool night air still fresh in my lungs, I stepped into the crowded house, feeling a renewed sense of calm. As I made my way to the dessert table, smiling faces turned to greet me, and I knew I was ready to mix, mingle, and maybe even make a few new friends.

Social Gatherings

Navigating informal social gatherings can feel like stepping into a whirlwind—loud groups of unfamiliar faces, the clamor of conversation, and that nagging urge to retreat to the safety of home. It's easy to feel overwhelmed and drained by the thought of having to chat brightly with multiple strangers. The temptation to skip these events entirely is strong, but avoiding parties, happy hours, or family reunions means missing out on unique opportunities to connect, build new relationships, and deepen old ones.

Saying no to these gatherings may protect us from temporary discomfort, but it also keeps us from the enriching experiences that come from stepping out of our comfort zones. By skipping out, we lose the chance to meet inspiring mentors, make new friends, or even reconnect with family. The good news? With a little practice, you can turn these nerve-wracking situations into opportunities for growth. Being around lively people expands your social comfort zone, much like exercising a muscle.

Be kind to yourself in the process. Growth doesn't happen overnight, and it's okay to take small steps out of your cocoon. Using a few simple tricks to ease social anxiety, you can gradually build confidence in these settings. Stepping into an informal social scene, like my neighbor's house party, might feel intimidating at first, but with the right approach, it can also be invigorating. Mingling with large, unfamiliar groups gathered for celebration rather than business presents unpredictability, but it also offers prime opportunities to stretch your social muscles if you approach them with intention.

After braving the initial vulnerability of walking into these vibrant exchanges, I've seen firsthand how applying a few confidence-building strategies can turn dreaded small talk into a refreshing exercise in connection. Here are some tips that will help you become more comfortable in social gatherings:

- **Arrive Early:** Getting to the party about 20-30 minutes after the official start time lets you ease into the event. Conversations are more relaxed before the peak, giving you time to warm up your social muscles gradually. Early arrivals also allow for more intimate chats before the room fills up, helping you feel more at ease as the crowd grows.

- **Offer to Help:** A great way to break the ice is by offering your assistance. Ask the host, "How can I help?" Most will gladly assign you a small task. If they don't, take the initiative—refill snack bowls, stir drinks, or tidy up. These small tasks keep your hands busy and create natural opportunities to interact with others, all while showing your appreciation for the host.

- **Bring an Icebreaker:** Bringing something that sparks conversation can make introductions smoother. Whether it's a favorite wine, a homemade appetizer, or a unique flower arrangement, these items invite natural comments and questions from others. Plus, they make for thoughtful hostess gifts, helping you start the evening on a positive note.

- **Listen Closely:** Meaningful connections start with good listening. Rather than jumping in to talk about yourself, ask guests thoughtful questions about their interests, what brought them to the event, or their favorite music or books. Listening attentively makes others feel valued and respected, which lays the groundwork for genuine relationships.

- **Offer Affirmations:** Spread good vibes by offering sincere compliments and positive feedback. Tell the hosts what you appreciate about the event, like their excellent music selection or the beautiful decor. Compliment new acquaintances on their insightful conversation or stylish outfits. These small acts of affirmation create a welcoming atmosphere, making everyone feel more comfortable and connected.

- **Match the Energy:** To blend seamlessly into the event, observe the room's general vibe and adjust your energy accordingly. If most guests are relaxed, follow suit. If the atmosphere is lively with dancing and games, bring a moderate level of enthusiasm to match. Aligning your energy with the crowd helps you fit in and enjoy the experience.

- **Recharge When Needed:** As fun as mingling can be, it's important to take breaks to avoid burnout. Find a quiet corner or step outside for a moment to re-center. This short pause helps you recharge, so you can rejoin the festivities feeling refreshed. Some of the best connections happen during these quiet moments—inviting someone to join you on the patio can lead to a more intimate and meaningful conversation.

- **Initiate Newcomer Connections:** Show empathy by reaching out to others who seem to be hovering at the edges of the event. A simple introduction can go a long way in helping them feel included. When I meet other introverts, I make it a point to introduce them to someone they might connect with. Even when standing alone, keep a smile on your face and avoid hiding behind your phone—this signals to others that you're open to meeting new people.

- **Say Yes to Group Activities:** Don't shy away from group activities like dancing, games, or karaoke. Saying yes to these opportunities often leads to laughter, memories, and bonding with others. Even if you're not keen on every activity, find something you can participate in—it's a great way to break the ice and make connections.

- **Extend Invitations:** If you hit it off with someone, don't hesitate to extend an invitation to meet again. Suggest exchanging numbers to grab coffee or lunch or to attend a local event together. This helps new friendships blossom beyond the initial meeting and keeps the connection alive.

Using these techniques, you can transform social gatherings from anxiety-inducing events into opportunities for genuine connection and enjoyable experiences. With practice, these strategies will help you feel more at ease, allowing you to fully engage in the lively, unpredictable world of social gatherings.

Networking Events

Networking events are professional gatherings designed to connect with others in your industry, build relationships, and open doors to new opportunities. These events aren't just about socializing—they're strategic occasions where you can meet mentors, potential clients, valuable insiders, and future partners.

In today's world, where careers are often built on connections, having a strong resume isn't always enough. Leveraging personal relationships can lead to learning about job opportunities before they're posted, getting referrals from influencers, advancing your career, or even securing startup funding. Networking is pivotal, and those who excel at it often climb the career ladder faster.

I've seen this firsthand. There was a young man who attended several networking events where my husband and I were present. Every time, he would greet my husband face-to-face with confidence, "You're supposed to be my mentor!" While I knew him as an acquaintance, my husband didn't know him very well. But after persistent, yet polite, requests, my husband finally agreed to a coffee meet-up. That conversation sparked a mentoring relationship that continues to this day.

When you set out to network, it's helpful to establish some goals. Decide how many meaningful conversations you want to have or how many business cards you aim to exchange before calling it a night. (And no, picking up a stray business card from the floor doesn't count—only real conversations do!) Setting these goals keeps you focused and ensures you stay in networking mode until you achieve them.

But let's be honest—smoothly working a room and leaving a great impression doesn't come naturally to everyone. That's where mastering small talk becomes essential. In these time-sensitive situations, you need to grab attention quickly and spark intrigue without wasting a moment. A few seconds of awkward silence or rambling nervously won't build the stellar reputation you're aiming for. Nailing first impressions and building instant rapport requires a bit of strategy.

Turning Brief Encounters into Valuable Connections

Skillful small talk is the bedrock of productive networking conversations. It's about capturing attention quickly, demonstrating likability, and credibly conveying your value before diving into deeper discussions. First impressions often set the tone for the entire relationship, so it's crucial to avoid awkward gaps and maintain a balance between sharing about yourself and showing interest in others. Here are some tips to help you excel at networking small talk:

- **Craft a Crisp Origin Story:** Have a 30-second overview of your current role, passions, and mission focus ready to share when someone asks, "What do you do?" This concise story helps you communicate clearly and leaves a lasting impression.

- **Research the Event and Attendees:** Before the event, take some time to scan the attendee list,

learn about the organizers, and familiarize yourself with the agenda topics. This preparation allows you to ask insightful questions and engage
in more meaningful conversations.

- **Initiate Conversations Gracefully:** When entering a new conversation, start with open-ended,
thoughtful questions about their day, their role,
or the causes they're passionate about. Listen in-
tently and make mental notes before gently shifting the focus to yourself.

- **Find Common Ground:** Look for mutual connections, shared associations, alma maters, or re-
gional ties. These shared elements help you bond
faster with your conversation partners and make
the dialogue flow more naturally. For example, I
had a friend who asked everyone he met if they
were acquainted with a certain executive he wanted to meet. Believe it or not, someone eventually
invited both him and the executive to lunch, fa-
cilitating a key introduction.

- **Balance Give and Take:** Avoid dominating the
conversation by constantly talking about yourself. After sharing your story, redirect the focus

to your conversation partner by asking about the issues that excite them.

- **Express Upbeat Optimism:** Smile, make moderate eye contact, and keep the discussion largely positive. Focus on progress and opportunities rather than dwelling on problems. This approach naturally attracts like-minded, optimistic people and helps you build a network of positive influencers.

- **Follow Your Curiosity:** Let your genuine curiosity guide your questions. If something about their work or experiences piques your interest—whether it's their leadership style, industry insights, or project challenges—ask more about it. This not only deepens the conversation but also shows that you're truly engaged.

- **Give Graceful Goodbyes:** When it's time to part ways, express your appreciation for the conversation. Highlight any shared passions, hand your card directly to the person, and specify when you'll follow up. This leaves a memorable, positive impression and keeps the door open for future interactions.

While it's important to stay on your feet and actively work the room, don't underestimate the value of taking a seat and connecting with those around you. Balancing mingling with moments of rest allows you to recharge while still making valuable connections. When you sit down—whether at a table or in a more casual seating area—you create an inviting space for others to join you. This often leads to deeper, more relaxed conversations that might not happen in the hustle of standing and moving around. So, don't be afraid to take a break from the crowd, rest your feet, and work the area around you. Sometimes, the most meaningful exchanges happen when you're comfortably seated, creating an opportunity for others to naturally gravitate toward you.

I did just this at a networking event held on a rooftop terrace. Many of the women had arrived straight from work, still in their high heels. One woman slid down onto the seat next to me and asked if she could join. We quickly bonded over the trials of painful but gorgeous footwear. It turned out she was the CEO of a local charity, and our connection has led to frequent reconnections at various meetings, including those hosted by her organization.

After the event, make it a habit to follow up with the people you met. For instance, the morning after, I often look up each person on LinkedIn and send a connection request with a personalized message: "We met at the Chamber of Commerce meeting last night at the mall, and I so enjoyed our conversation. I wanted to connect with you here and hope we can talk again soon." This message not only jogs their memory but also records the event's details for future reference, helping me maintain and nurture those new connections.

Networking conversations are a delicate balance of sharing your story and learning from others. When both parties reveal something meaningful—whether its challenges to overcome or hopes for the future—bonds are formed that can lead to lasting, cooperative ventures. With these tips in your toolkit, you'll be well on your way to turning brief encounters into valuable connections.

Professional Settings

Navigating small talk in the workplace can be a delicate balancing act. In professional settings like offices, conferences, job sites, or leadership retreats, communication tends to focus on productivity rather than casual chit-chat. These environments are often structured by formal hierarchies, rules, and behavioral norms that influence how conversations unfold.

How Professional Settings Shape Small Talk

The nature of workplace interactions naturally impacts how small talk plays out. Here are a few key ways these environments shape casual conversations:

- **Narrower Range of Topics:** In professional settings, some subjects are best avoided. Confidential work matters, controversial issues, or personal intimate details aren't suitable for light conversation. Instead, safe topics like sports, popular media, food, or weekend plans dominate the casual banter. These topics help maintain a comfortable and professional atmosphere.

- **Shorter Conversations:** Time is often a precious commodity in the workplace, so small talk is typically brief. Quick chats by the coffee machine, a few friendly exchanges before a meeting, or a brief conversation while waiting for a conference call to start are common. These interactions are kept short, especially when deadlines are looming, ensuring that productivity remains high.

- **Awareness of Hierarchy:** In professional environments, the etiquette around hierarchy is crucial. For example, staff members might avoid making overly familiar jokes with executives, and managers typically refrain from delving too deeply into the personal lives of their team members. Being mindful of status and appropriate boundaries is key to maintaining respect and professionalism.

- **Networking as a Goal:** In many professional settings, small talk often serves a strategic purpose—building relationships that could benefit your career. Whether you're trying to make a good impression on a potential mentor, client, or colleague, small talk becomes a tool for gently marketing yourself and establishing valuable connections.

To navigate these professional settings effectively, it's important to avoid overly personal or critical disclosures that could overstep unwritten boundaries. Instead, focus on conversations that support your career, enhance your reputation, and help you climb the organizational ladder. Mastering this balance will enable you to make a strong impression and build meaningful professional relationships.

Making Small Talk in the Workplace

Engaging in small talk with coworkers around the office can be tricky. You want to be friendly but keep it professional. Here are some simple tips to help you strike the right balance:

- **Start with Polite Greetings:** A warm "Good morning!" or "Happy Monday" can set a positive tone for the day and help you connect with colleagues in a friendly way.

- **Ask Safe, Friendly Questions:** Questions like, "How was your weekend?" or "Got any fun plans coming up?" show that you're interested in your coworkers without getting too personal.

- **Comment on Shared Experiences:** Brief comments on topics you have in common—like the weather, office news, or the latest cafeteria offerings—can help bridge gaps without crossing any lines.

- **Avoid Controversial Topics:** Steer clear of discussions around politics or religion unless you're certain it's safe. Stick to topics like pets, movies, or sports, which are generally less divisive. For example, I'm known as someone who prays, so coworkers often ask me to pray for them—but I'm careful not to initiate those conversations.

- **Listen More Than You Speak:** Let your coworkers share their thoughts and ideas, and avoid dominating the conversation with your own stories.

- Ask Thoughtful Questions: If you're unsure what to talk about, ask colleagues about their current projects, workflows, or other non-private aspects of their roles. This invites them to guide the conversation while keeping it professional.

Meaningful Conversations During an Interview

Interviews can be nerve-wracking, but there's more to success than just reciting rehearsed answers. Here's how to connect more deeply during an interview:

- **Actively Listen:** Pay close attention when interviewers talk about the role, company culture, and leadership philosophies. Reflect on what they've said when you respond to demonstrate genuine interest.

- **Ask Insightful Questions:** Show that you're engaged by asking intelligent questions about details that stood out to you, like company values, training programs, or typical workflows. Follow your curiosity to dive deeper into topics that matter to you.

- **Share Examples, Not Just Statements:** When asked about your qualifications, provide examples from past jobs that illustrate your competencies. For instance, instead of saying, "I'm an excellent team player," share a story about how you united colleagues on a project.

- **Research the Company:** Before the interview, research the company's latest news and projects. Ask thoughtful questions that reflect your knowledge, such as, "I read about the new product your team recently launched. How has the market response been?"

- **Compliment Their Achievements:** Show that you admire the company's work by complimenting recent achievements. For example, "I'm impressed by how you shifted to a more ecological manufacturing process last year. How has that impacted the company culture?"

- **Find Personal Common Ground:** Look for ways to bond over shared interests. For example, "I noticed an employee hiking club in the office photos. I just went on a great hike last weekend in the Cascades!"

- **Inquire About Work-Life Balance:** Ask questions that reflect your interest in a healthy work-life balance, such as, "What wellness benefits or work schedules make it feasible here for busy parents?"

- **Give Vivid, Colorful Answers:** When answering questions, illustrate your skills with detailed examples. For instance, "I collaborated closely across teams when launching our rebranded website. I still grab coffee occasionally with those designers and marketers."

Balancing professionalism with warmth is key during interviews. Avoid overly personal details, but don't be afraid to show your friendly, human side. Share your genuine excitement about contributing your talents to support the company's goals.

After every interview, I always follow up with both an email and a handwritten letter thanking the interviewer for their time and expressing my interest in the role. These notes arrive at different times, doubling the impact and helping me stand out from other applicants. Few people take this extra step, and it really makes a difference.

As you navigate through the varied landscapes of social gatherings, networking events, and professional settings, remember that the key to mastering small talk lies in your ability to adapt. Each environment presents its own challenges and opportunities, but with the right mindset and tools, you can turn every interaction into a meaningful connection.

Adaptability is your superpower. It's what allows you to move confidently from a casual conversation at a neighborhood party to a strategic exchange at a networking event, and then to a professional discussion in the workplace. By staying attuned to the nuances of each setting, you can tailor your approach, engage authentically, and leave a lasting impression.

But don't forget—this is a journey. You won't get everything perfect right away, and that's okay. The more you practice, the more these skills will become second nature. Each conversation, whether it's a brief chat in the office kitchen or an in-depth discussion during an interview, is an opportunity to learn, grow, and refine your approach.

So, step into each situation with confidence, knowing that you have the tools to adapt, connect, and thrive. Embrace the diversity of interactions that life offers, and let your adaptability guide you to new relationships, career opportunities, and personal growth. The conversations you have today are the building blocks of the connections that will shape your future.

Remember, every word you speak is a chance to make a positive impact. Use your voice, your adaptability, and your unique perspective to enrich the lives of those around you—and in doing so, you'll enrich your own.

Reflections & Practice

LET'S GET HANDS-ON AND apply these concepts to real situations so you can nail social and professional conversations with way more ease and eloquence! After we cover communication fundamentals together, I'll walk through exercises I guide my coaching clients through.

1. Plan conversation starters for an upcoming social event

For an upcoming baby shower, wedding, conference, or whatever, envision who will be there and what common contexts you share ahead of time. Now craft open-ended yet intriguing questions for various acquaintances referencing shared knowledge as automatic ice breakers. Here are some examples to get you started.

- What dish did you bring to share? It looks delicious!

- This playlist is fun - what music have you been enjoying lately?

- How do you know the hosts? Did you go to college together?

- Have you been to any good concerts or shows recently?

- Caught highlights of the game last night? What do you think?

- Have you tried that new bakery down the block? Killer pastries.

Example for book club friends: "Hi Maggie! I loved that author's latest novel—such an unpredictable twist ending! If she were here tonight, what's one literary question you'd be dying to ask her over appetizers?" This instantly resumes your last chat while inviting deeper discussion.

See how easy it is to initiate conversations by referencing common knowledge or reputations? Now, try crafting a few starter lines for upcoming encounters.

2. List appropriate small talk topics for your workplace.

Keeping office chitchat light avoids wrecking work relationships that appear overly personal. Run potential subjects through this checklist:

- Neutral current events

- Upcoming department activities

- Aligning workflows

- Weekend/holiday plans (briefly)

- Harmless personal interests, like sports teams, TV shows, books, and food

As you can see, workplace-wise pros steer conversations, staying job-related or focused on harmless trivia, building camaraderie. Now, brainstorm safe topics for your next coffee break!

For unfamiliar new work contacts, it may sound more like: "Hi, Sue from Marketing, right? I don't think we've met in person yet. Quick question—what's the must-see exhibit your team has up this year? My niece can't stop raving about last year's awesome tech lounge you all hosted!" This breaks the ice by touting others' accomplishments while inquiring about coveted details.

3. Make a list of your strengths for an interview.

Humble bragging in interviews is crucial! We must highlight achievements, skills, and values, illustrating our cultural fit and talents aligned to requisites without sounding cocky. Review the job description marking required competencies, then reflect on authentic examples from your experience exemplifying those in action:

Recount success stories. Describe in detail how you solved a problem where you worked previously. If you have numbers to back up your achievements, like percentages, profit improvements, etc., highlight those as well.

Align your origin story to position strengths as solutions for the role's core issues to showcase a match. Now draft yours!

4. List your weaknesses, then spin them positively for an interview.

I once tanked a job interview with the cliche "I'm too much of a perfectionist!" response revealing insecurity, not excellence striving. Never confess actual performance gaps or habits sabotaging productivity. Instead, reframe improvement areas as continuing growth opportunities:

"I'm energized diving deeply into data analysis, occasionally losing sight of time before realizing the meeting starts in five minutes!" This shows you get engrossed in producing great work while reassuring you are adjusting your time management.

I love quickly changing and adapting to business procedures and software changes, so sometimes, I get bored with the same old routine. You flip honest struggles to showcase lessons, accelerating responsibilities you handle smoothly.

Let's reword your imperfections into answers positioning you as proactive, coachable, and responsible rather than flawed.

5. Develop a strategy for making meaningful connections at a networking event.

We covered this above, so now it's time for you to plan your next networking event. How many connections do you want to make? How long do you want to stay? How will you make connections?

Map out how you will approach others and start conversations. Will you approach people standing alone? Or will you slide into groups whose body language indicates they'd welcome more people into the conversation?

Whew, you nailed it, my friend! Do you feel more equipped now to steer any social or professional conversation tactfully? It just takes planning and practice. Your abilities will strengthen the more you engage across scenarios. I'm cheering you on.

We just covered a ton of ground unpacking how to adapt your communication style flexibly based on the situation, whether parties, interviews, work meetings, or more. Here comes the fun part. Now, we get to focus on initial impressions—how to absolutely wow strangers you want to woo as contacts within the first minute or two of interacting.

You already have ample skills to hold your own in diverse settings. But let's build your foundation to a point where others remember you and your pitch, as well as you remember theirs. We want you to be MEMORABLE!

Chapter 7

Making a Positive Impression

IN THE EARLY DAYS of my career, I remember feeling a bit out of my depth at large networking mixers. My extroverted husband would dive into the crowd, effortlessly connecting with everyone, while I preferred to observe from the sidelines, taking it all in.

But what I've learned over the years is that even the most reserved among us can develop the skills to make confident, positive impressions. It's not about changing who you are, but about harnessing your unique strengths to connect with others in meaningful ways.

In this chapter, we'll explore the key techniques I've honed to navigate mixers and events with ease, turning those initial encounters into lasting, supportive professional relationships. Whether you're naturally outgoing or more reserved, these strategies will help you leave a memorable mark on every new connection.

First Impressions

The first minute of a meeting often shapes how someone perceives you, and as they say, first impressions stick. Making a positive impact right from the start can set the tone for a comfortable and productive conversation.

One of the easiest ways to make a great first impression is by confidently introducing yourself. I've found that being at ease with saying my name and company name goes a long way in creating a positive connection. It's a simple but powerful skill that everyone should master. Practice introducing yourself until it feels natural: "Hi, I'm [your first and last name] with [your company name]." Try rehearsing this in front of a mirror until it becomes second nature.

Next, greet newcomers warmly by name, paired with a genuine, confident smile. A handshake is more than just a formality—briefly cradling their hand between yours can convey warmth and sincerity. Align your body subtly with theirs, and make sure your words reflect an understanding of their priorities.

This balanced, nonverbal approach puts others at ease and positions you as someone worth knowing—an emotionally intelligent leader rather than just another busi-

ness card. The tips below will help you express genuine
interest in under sixty seconds, laying the groundwork for
meaningful business relationships that last well beyond
the initial meeting.

Ways to Deliver Dynamite First Impressions

We've all heard the saying, "You never get a second chance
to make a first impression," and while that might sound
like a lot of pressure, it doesn't have to be. Making a dynamite first impression is less about perfection and more
about being authentic, approachable, and a little bit prepared. Here are some tried-and-true ways to make sure
you're remembered for all the right reasons:

1. **Own Your Introduction:** You know how sometimes you introduce yourself, and it feels like
   you're just going through the motions? Let's
   change that. When you say, "Hi, I'm [your name]
   with [your company]," say it like you're genuinely
   excited about who you are and what you do. Your
   enthusiasm is contagious and makes others excited to meet you.

2. **Smile Like You Mean It:** A smile is your secret
   weapon. It's the quickest way to put people at ease
   and show that you're friendly and approachable.

But here's the key—make sure your smile reaches your eyes. A genuine smile is more than just lips; it's an invitation to connect.

3. **Give a Handshake, not a Power Play:** We've all experienced those handshakes that feel like a wrestling match. Don't be that person. Aim for a handshake that's firm but friendly. Think Goldilocks: It's not too hard, not too soft, and just right. And if you're comfortable, briefly cradle their hand between yours to add a touch of warmth.

4. **Mirror, Mirror:** Subtly aligning your body language with the person you're speaking to can create an instant connection. It's like saying, "Hey, we're on the same page." But remember, subtly is key—no one likes a mime. Just a slight adjustment to your stance or tone can work wonders.

5. **Say Their Name and Say It Again:** People love hearing their own name—it's like music to their ears. Use it when you greet them and try to weave it into the conversation a couple of times. It shows you're paying attention and helps cement that connection. Just don't overdo it—you're aiming

for smooth jazz, not a drum solo.

6. **Show Genuine Interest:** This one's a game-changer. Ask questions that show you're truly interested in the person you're talking to. And here's the kicker—actually listen to their answers. Respond with follow-up questions or comments that prove you're engaged. There's nothing more impressive than someone who listens with intent.

7. **Keep It Positive:** We all have those days, but when you're making a first impression, leave the negativity at the door. Focus on the good stuff—what's working, what's exciting, what's new. Positivity is magnetic, and people will remember you as someone who brought good energy into the room.

8. **Be Confident, Not Cocky:** Confidence is attractive, but there's a fine line between confidence and arrogance. Share your accomplishments with pride, but also show humility. People appreciate someone who knows their worth without needing to boast about it.

9. **Wrap It Up with Gratitude:** Before you move on to the next person, wrap up your conversation with a sincere thank you. Whether it's thanking them for their time, their insights, or just for chatting with you, ending on a note of gratitude leaves a lasting impression of warmth and appreciation.

Remember, making a dynamite first impression isn't about dazzling others with perfection—it's about being your authentic, likable self. So, go out there, flash that smile, give a great handshake, and leave a trail of positive impressions wherever you go.

The key to making these impressions last lies in preparation. By aligning your capabilities with their needs ahead of time, you'll find that interactions flow naturally. Confidently and humbly lead conversations with a focus on solutions and allyship. Even small tweaks to your approach can significantly elevate the impact you make.

Avoiding Common Mistakes in Your Personal Introduction

Crafting a memorable fifteen-second personal introduction can be tricky, but avoiding these common pitfalls will set you on the right path:

- **Rambling without a clear point:** Long, winding introductions quickly lose people's interest. Have a crisp, compelling headline statement ready to draw attention right from the start.

- **Overloading with too many details:** There's no need to cram your entire backstory into fifteen seconds. Focus on the most relevant accomplishments and passions that align with the context of the meeting.

- **Forgetting to restate your name:** Don't assume they caught your name during the initial chatter. Clearly state your name and profession upfront to ensure they know who you are.

- **Making it all about you:** While it's important to share key details about yourself, remember to show genuine interest in the person you're speaking with. Balance is key.

- **Failing to tie back to the event:** Context matters. Reference how your goals align with the event's themes and community to show you're engaged and purposeful in your presence.

• **Speaking unclearly or too quietly:** Nerves can get the best of us, but it's crucial to speak slowly, make eye contact, and project your voice with confidence.

- **Ending awkwardly without a question:** Wrap up your introduction by asking an open-ended question that demonstrates your interest in their work, perspectives, or advice. This shifts the conversation into a meaningful exchange.

Crafting a strong introduction in the first minute sets the tone for the conversations that follow. Start by clearly stating your full name and profession, making it easy for them to grasp who you are. Summarize your niche specialization in a few concise, intriguing sentences that highlight what energizes you most professionally.

To create a connection quickly, blend facts about your background with a glimpse of your personal passions—whether it's volcano climbing or rescuing stray dogs on weekends! Close your thirty-second sound bite with a compelling statistic or quote tied to innovations in your niche. This not only hooks their curiosity but also positions you as an ideally suited collaborator for advancing shared goals.

Finally, wrap up with an open-ended question to shift the focus to them, inviting a lively exchange that helps you grasp their vision and values. By balancing these elements—your name, profession, key data, passion points, and inclusive questions—you'll craft introductions that stick, setting you apart and paving the way for meaningful connections.

Demonstrating Empathy & Understanding

I've learned that lively small talk truly begins with showing genuine care and empathy, which often comes from being curious about other people's worlds. Before diving into a conversation, it's crucial to tune in and understand the context—it's the foundation of building rapport through empathy.

In the past, I'd often find myself on the outskirts of sophisticated social circles, listening in but hesitating to contribute. I wasn't sure how to join the conversation smoothly, so I'd often stay quiet rather than risk saying something out of sync with the group. Over time, I realized that meaningful conversations start with active listening. By tuning into the current topic and understanding the flow of the discussion, I could find the right moment to add my voice.

 Now, I make it a point to listen and observe before jumping in. I pay attention to what excites people—whether it's a deep dive into South African politics or a passionate discussion about avant-garde art.

When I do contribute, I ensure my comments reflect what's already been shared, whether that's through expressing admiration or offering a related experience. Even in the most serious discussions, a genuine compliment or a thoughtful question can open the door to a deeper connection, turning a potentially intimidating exchange into a meaningful dialogue.

Remember, you don't have to fake comprehension right away. People appreciate honesty and are usually open to new ideas once they see that you're genuinely engaged and curious, not combative or close-minded. From there, unscripted and meaningful dialogues can unfold, leading to new understandings for everyone involved.

Here are some practical ways to build rapport through empathy in conversations:

1. **Spotlight Shared Values: When someone mentions a cause important to them, highlight how your values align. This shared con-**

nection lays the foundation for deeper rapport.

- **Them:** "I volunteer at the animal shelter when I can. Helping those poor pups breaks my heart but fills it, too."

- **You:** "I'm passionate about animal welfare, too. It's so meaningful that you dedicate your time to help them."

2. Express Encouragement: Celebrate their accomplishments or dreams, and emphasize how inspiring their efforts are—regardless of how flashy the impact might be.

o **Them:** "I finally opened my own bakery this year after so many attempts!"

o **You:** "That's amazing! It takes so much courage and resilience to get a small business off the ground."

3. Explore Their Origins: Ask how they got started on their path to uncover the experiences that shaped their perspective. This invites deeper compassion.

o **Them:** "I became a doctor because my little sister struggled with a scary illness when we were young."

o **You:** "I can imagine those experiences really shaped your approach to patient care. How did that influence your decision to pursue medicine?"

4. Discuss Their Growth Process: When someone mentions progress, dig into their journey rather than just the end result. How have they developed resilience, wisdom, and vision over time?

o **Them:** "I directed my first play last year! It felt like a surreal milestone after years of hard work."

o **You:** "That's incredible! What strengths and support helped you through the highs and lows leading up to opening night?"

5. Allow Some Mystery Initially: Early on, keep things light and focus on finding points of connection and appreciation. Depth can come later.

o **Them:** "I'm pouring everything into getting my non-profit for Ocean Literacy off the ground!"

o **You:** "Your vision is so inspiring! I'd love to exchange ideas again once you've got some solid footing."

6. Note Resilience Factors: If they mention setbacks, highlight the strengths and strategies they used to persevere. This reinforces their agency.

o **Them:** "The pandemic nearly sank my new restaurant. We had to pivot to takeout just to stay afloat."

o **You:** "It's impressive how quickly you adapted! What resources or support helped you navigate such a challenging time?"

7. Share Helpful Resources: Only offer recommendations after you fully understand their situation. Tailor your advice to meet them where they are.

o **Them:** "I'm overwhelmed juggling full-time work and nursing school..."

o **You:** "That sounds intense! Once I understand your program better, I'd love to share any study or self-care resources that might ease the load."

8. Express Unconditional Positive Regard: Like in counseling, show respect and acceptance regardless of their actions. Let go of judgment.

o **Them:** "I'm so frustrated—I relapsed into an old habit after doing so well."

o **You:** "It's great that you recognized it quickly. Everyone stumbles, but the courage to start over is what matters. How can I support you?"

9. Demonstrate Engaged Body Language: Show that you care through nonverbal signals—turn toward them, make eye contact, nod, and smile.

o **Them:** Shoulders hunched, frequently checking their phone.

o **You:** Lean in with a smile and full eye contact, "I really appreciate you taking the time to catch up today."

10. Clarify Next Steps: When the conversation is winding down, summarize key points and suggest meeting again if it could lead to further meaningful collaboration.

• **Them:** "I'm thinking about quitting my job to pursue music full-time."

• **You:** "It sounds like chasing that dream really aligns with your passion. Let's plan to meet up next month to discuss practical steps for making it happen."

The more you allow mutual understanding to unfold, the richer the opportunities for connection become. Lead with your heart, and everything else will fall into place. By shifting from transactional talk to transformational dialogue, you lay the groundwork for authentic relationships that are built on empathy and understanding.

Using Humor in Small Talk

Humor is one of the most effective tools in the small talk toolkit. It breaks the ice, eases tension, and helps you connect with others on a more personal level. But using humor in conversation isn't about being the next stand-up comedian—it's about finding lightness in the moment and sharing it with others.

The beauty of humor is that it can turn even the most mundane topics into something memorable. A well-timed

joke or a light-hearted comment can make you more approachable and help others feel at ease. The key is to keep
it natural—don't force it. Humor should flow from the
conversation, not feel like an unrelated punchline dropped
into the mix.

Here are a few tips for using humor effectively in small
talk:

1. **Keep it Light:** Small talk isn't the place for
   edgy or controversial jokes. Stick to humor that's
   universally relatable—think funny observations
   about everyday life or light-hearted comments
   that everyone can enjoy.

2. **Self-Deprecation, In Moderation:** A bit of
   self-deprecating humor can make you seem more
   down-to-earth and relatable. However, it's important not to overdo it. You want to come across
   as confident and self-aware, not as someone who's
   constantly putting themselves down.

3. **Read the Room:** Pay attention to how your humor is received. If people are laughing and smiling, great! If not, it might be time to switch gears.
   Not every attempt at humor will land, and that's
   okay. The goal is to connect, not to deliver a perfect joke every time.

4. **Share a Funny Anecdote:** Sharing a brief, funny story about something that happened to you can be a great way to lighten the mood and give others a glimpse of your personality. Just keep it short and relevant to the conversation at hand.

5. **Be Authentic:** The best humor comes from being yourself. Don't feel like you have to perform or be someone you're not. Share what genuinely makes you laugh, and others will likely find it funny too.

6. **Know When to Dial it Back:** Humor can be a powerful tool, but it's important to balance it with sincerity. Too much joking around can make it hard for others to take you seriously when the conversation shifts to more important topics. Know when to switch from humor to a more serious tone.

Humor is a bridge that connects people, making conversations more enjoyable and memorable. When used thoughtfully, it can transform small talk from a simple exchange of words into a shared experience that leaves everyone smiling.

Lightening the Mood Appropriately

We've all been there—moments when a conversation starts to feel a bit heavy, tense, or just plain awkward. Knowing how to lighten the mood can make a world of difference, helping to steer the conversation back to a more comfortable and enjoyable place. Here's how to do it with a touch of finesse:

Humor as a Reset: If things are getting too intense, a light-hearted comment or quick joke can reset the tone. For example, in the middle of a stressful work discussion, you might quip, "At least we're not tackling this on a Monday morning!" It's a simple way to ease the tension without downplaying the topic.

Shifting to a Lighter Topic: Sometimes, the conversation just needs a change of scenery. If you sense the mood dipping, gently steer the discussion toward something more upbeat. For instance, "Speaking of challenges, have you caught the latest episode of [popular show]? It really had me on the edge of my seat!" This keeps things moving while introducing a lighter note.

Acknowledge and Pivot: When a conversation gets a bit too deep, acknowledge the seriousness before transitioning. You might say, "That sounds like a lot to handle—I'm impressed with how you're managing it. On a lighter note, what are your plans for the weekend?" This shows empathy while gracefully shifting the tone.

Playful Banter: Playful teasing—when done with care and someone you know well—can diffuse tension. For example, if a colleague is stressing about a presentation, you might smile and say, "You're going to knock it out of the park—no pressure or anything!" Just be sure the person is comfortable with this kind of interaction.

Sharing a Positive Anecdote: A brief, positive story from your own life can also lighten the mood. If the conversation has turned serious, you might say, "That reminds me of a time when I was in a similar situation, and something unexpectedly great happened..." This not only brightens the mood but also adds a personal touch.

Knowing When to Hold Back: Sometimes, lightening the mood isn't the right approach—especially if someone is sharing something deeply personal or serious. In these moments, being a compassionate listener is more important than trying to change the tone. Offering support and empathy is what really matters.

Lightening the mood appropriately is about being in tune with the conversation and the people you're with. It's a skill that, when used thoughtfully, can make interactions more enjoyable and help build stronger connections. Remember, it's not about avoiding the tough topics but rather about knowing when and how to add a touch of lightness to keep the conversation balanced and engaging.

Making a positive impression is more than just a momentary win—it's the foundation for building lasting, meaningful connections. Whether you're navigating a networking event, engaging in small talk at a social gathering, or simply meeting someone for the first time, the way you present yourself leaves an indelible mark.

Remember, it's not about perfection. It's about being genuine, showing empathy, and bringing a touch of humor and lightness to every interaction. When you approach each conversation with authenticity and a sincere desire to connect, you create a ripple effect that goes beyond just that one moment. You open doors to new opportunities, strengthen your relationships, and build a reputation that speaks volumes about who you are.

So, as you move forward, carry these lessons with you. Embrace the power of first impressions, the importance of empathy, and the joy of lightening the mood when needed. Let your interactions be a reflection of your true self—confident, compassionate, and always ready to make a difference in the lives of those you meet.

Every conversation is an opportunity to leave a lasting legacy. Make each one count.

Reflections & Practice

1. WRITE DOWN TECHNIQUES for making a strong initial impact.

Remember, we talked about ways to make a positive first impression. Just make a list of things you plan to try this week, then start another list to try next week. This chapter will keep giving you great ideas until you are a natural!

2. Practice empathetic responses in conversations. Note the difference it makes in that interaction.

Connecting with others starts with understanding their perspective and experiences. I'm learning to listen more closely to the underlying verbal and nonverbal meanings. Thoughtful, validating responses demonstrate genuine care and concern. Jot down some difficult conversations you remember, then practice your empathetic responses. Here are some examples to get you started:

• A coworker shares about a frustrating work situation.

• A friend shares some struggles with the relationship with their spouse.

• A leader discusses low morale issues in the company.

3, Brainstorm light and appropriate jokes or humorous comments for different scenarios.

Light humor can spark warmer conversations once initial rapport is built. Witty quips exchanged back and forth help both parties relax and not take things too seriously. I mostly use humor about myself and what I do because I feel that's so safe, and it keeps me from becoming overly self-conscious. Make a short list!

The ability to make positive first impressions through strong introductions, showing genuine empathy, and using appropriate humor serves us well in widening social circles or deepening existing bonds. When conversations unfold quickly, feeling mutually uplifting for all parties involved motivates continual engagement and nourishing relationships in the long term.

While no one becomes beloved simply by employing a few conversational techniques alone and absent authentic care for people themselves, practicing intentional skills can strengthen the impact when connecting face-to-face initially. So, reflect on any area needing polishing up over time by paying thoughtful attention in interactions.

Having honed better habits of making memorable impressions one conversation at a time, how do we gain insights by scanning the entire dynamics of the environments we enter? Let's roll on to Chapter 8 – Reading Social Cues.

Chapter 8

Reading Social Cues

REMEMBER HOW I MENTIONED feeling super uncomfortable at networking events and parties? Well, it turns out I was making it out to be worse than it was—I wasn't nearly as out of place as I thought. What I really needed was a boost in confidence and a better understanding of social dynamics. I realized that to overcome the fear of judgment, I had to get better at reading the social cues others were giving me. Back then, every conversation felt a bit like walking on eggshells—disjointed and awkward.

However, as I continued to grow in my career and entrepreneurial journey, I quickly learned that building connections was vital to success. To achieve that easy rapport with new crowds, I needed to master the art of "reading the room." And unexpectedly, a bit of simple theater vocabulary provided the lifeline I needed, shedding light on everyday interactions in ways I hadn't imagined.

I came to realize that nonverbal body language and tone of voice are like the secret subtitles to any conversation, offering clues about what's really happening beyond the words being spoken. I didn't need to fake it anymore—I just needed to observe the signals that were already there. So, I started paying close attention to those who seemed naturally good at socializing. Before long, by following their lead, things began to click for me, too.

With dedicated practice, you can also navigate interactions smoothly by picking up on the cues in body language, verbal statements, and vocal tones that reveal underlying meanings. It's all about shifting your focus to notice those often overlooked but telling details and understanding whether connections are flowing smoothly or hitting a snag.

So, let's dive in: To get better at reading social cues, we need to start with body language. Just like watching an orchestra conductor cue musicians into harmony, we can learn to "conduct" ourselves by observing how others move and respond, finding our own rhythm in the social flow.

Understanding Body Language

Have you ever walked into a room and immediately sensed the mood, even before anyone spoke? That's the power of body language at work. It's often said that communication is more than just words—our bodies constantly send out signals that reveal our true feelings, intentions, and attitudes. Whether we're aware of it or not, body language is a major part of how we connect with others.

Think of body language as the silent conductor in the orchestra of conversation. While the words you say are the notes on the sheet music, it's your body language that sets the tempo, volume, and emotion. When we learn to understand these nonverbal cues, we gain a powerful tool to enhance our communication skills and deepen our connections with others.

The beauty of body language is that it's universal on many levels—smiles, eye contact, and open gestures are often recognized across cultures as signs of warmth and approachability. But there's also nuance; a slight shift in posture, a fleeting expression, or the way someone positions themselves can speak volumes about what they're really thinking or feeling.

In this section, we'll dive into the fascinating world of body language. We'll explore how to read the signals others are sending, how to become more aware of the messages your own body is conveying, and how to use this knowledge to navigate social interactions with greater ease and confidence.

The Importance of Body Language

Body language is the unsung hero of communication. While words carry the explicit message, body language often carries the emotional truth. It's said that up to 93% of communication is nonverbal—think about that for a moment. The way you stand, the look in your eyes, the subtle gestures you make—these all speak volumes before you even open your mouth.

When you understand body language, you're not just hearing what someone says; you're seeing what they feel. This can be the difference between a conversation that falls flat and one that resonates. For instance, someone might say they're "fine," but their slouched posture, lack of eye contact, and crossed arms might tell a different story. By picking up on these cues, you can respond with empathy and insight, leading to deeper and more meaningful connections.

But body language isn't just about reading others—it's also about how you present yourself. Your own body language can influence how others perceive you, even before you've had a chance to speak. A confident stance, a warm smile, and a relaxed demeanor can make you seem more approachable and trustworthy, setting the stage for positive interactions.

Body language is a powerful tool in both personal and professional settings. Whether you're meeting someone for the first time, negotiating a deal, or simply catching up with a friend, being attuned to nonverbal cues can help you navigate the conversation more effectively. It's about more than just understanding others—it's about mastering the art of communication in its entirety.

Common Body Language Cues

Now that we've established how important body language is, let's get into some of the most common cues you'll encounter—and what they're really saying. Think of these as the "greatest hits" of nonverbal communication, the signals that pop up in almost every interaction.

    1. **Posture:** How someone holds themselves can tell you a lot about their current state of mind. Standing tall with shoulders back? That's a clas-

sic sign of confidence. Slouching or shrinking into themselves? They might be feeling insecure, tired, or just plain uninterested. Next time you're chatting, take a quick mental note of your posture—standing tall not only makes you look more confident, but it can also help you feel more confident too.

2. **Facial Expressions:** We've all heard the saying, "The eyes are the windows to the soul," but really, it's the whole face that gives the game away. A genuine smile reaches the eyes, causing those little crinkles we sometimes call "laugh lines." A furrowed brow or a clenched jaw? That might mean someone is stressed or deep in thought. And remember, it's not just about reading others—being aware of your own expressions can help you convey the right emotions in any situation.

3. **Eye Contact:** Eye contact is one of the most powerful tools in communication. Too little, and you might come across as disinterested or evasive; too much, and you could seem intense or even intimidating. The sweet spot? A comfortable, natural level of eye contact that says, "I'm here, I'm listening, and I'm engaged." It's like Goldilocks—just

right.

4. **Gestures:** Gestures can add flavor to your words, but they can also stand on their own as powerful signals. Open gestures, like showing your palms, suggest honesty and openness, while closed gestures, like crossing your arms, can signal defensiveness or discomfort. And let's not forget about those unintentional gestures—fidgeting with a pen or tapping your foot might be your body's way of saying, "I'm anxious" or "I'm ready to move on."

5. **Proximity:** The distance we keep from others speaks volumes. Standing too close can feel invasive, while too much distance might suggest disinterest or discomfort. Finding the right balance is key—respecting personal space while also being close enough to show you're engaged. In most cases, an arm's length apart is a good rule of thumb for casual conversations.

6. **Touch:** Touch can be a powerful way to connect, but it's one of those things where context is everything. A light touch on the arm can convey warmth and empathy, but overdoing it or using

it in the wrong setting can make people uncomfortable. Always be mindful of the situation and the other person's comfort level.

Understanding these common body language cues is like learning a new language—one that's spoken silently but powerfully in every interaction. By becoming more attuned to these signals, you'll find that your conversations flow more naturally, and your connections deepen. And as you start to notice these cues in others, you'll also become more aware of the signals you're sending out into the world.

Mirroring and Matching

One of the most powerful yet subtle ways to build rapport with others is through mirroring and matching their body language. This doesn't mean copying someone like a mime—it's about reflecting their posture, gestures, and even tone of voice in a way that feels natural and comfortable. When done right, mirroring can create a sense of connection and mutual understanding, making conversations flow more smoothly.

What is Mirroring? Mirroring is the art of subtly matching the body language of the person you're interacting with. If they're leaning in, you might lean in slightly too. If they're using animated hand gestures, you might mirror that energy with your own gestures. This technique works because it signals to the other person that you're on the same wavelength, fostering a sense of trust and rapport.

Why It Works. Humans are wired to respond positively to people who are like them—it's part of what makes social bonds so strong. When you mirror someone's body language, you're essentially speaking their "nonverbal language," which can make them feel more comfortable and understood. It's like saying, "I get you," without uttering a word.

How to Use It. Mirroring is most effective when it's done naturally. Start by observing the other person's body language—are they sitting with their legs crossed? Are they speaking with enthusiasm? Then, without being too obvious, match their posture or energy level. The key is to keep it subtle and avoid making it seem like you're mimicking them, which can come off as insincere or even awkward.

A Word of Caution. While mirroring can be a great way to build rapport, it's important to use it judiciously. If done too overtly, it can feel forced or even creepy. The goal is to create a comfortable and natural connection, not to mirror every move the other person makes. Pay attention to how they respond—if they seem to relax and engage more, you're on the right track.

Benefits Beyond Rapport. Mirroring doesn't just help in casual conversations—it's a valuable skill in professional settings too. Whether you're in a job interview, a networking event, or negotiating a deal, mirroring can help you build a positive connection quickly. It's a silent signal that says, "We're on the same team," making it easier to collaborate and find common ground.

By incorporating mirroring and matching into your interactions, you'll find that building rapport becomes almost effortless. It's a subtle yet powerful way to connect with others on a deeper level, ensuring that your conversations are more engaging and mutually rewarding.

The Power of Personal Space

Personal space is one of those silent signals that can make or break a conversation. We all have an invisible bubble around us, and being aware of how close you get—or how far you stand—can play a big role in how comfortable the other person feels.

Finding the Right Balance. Respecting someone's personal space helps create a comfortable atmosphere. Standing too close might make them feel uneasy while keeping too much distance could make you seem aloof or disinterested. The key is to find that sweet spot where both of you feel at ease.

Reading the Signals. Watch for cues that indicate someone's comfort level with proximity. If they step back or angle their body away, it might be a sign to give them a little more space. On the other hand, if they lean in or move closer, it's a good indication they're engaged and comfortable.

Adjusting to the Situation. Remember, personal space isn't a one-size-fits-all concept. The context—whether you're at a networking event, in a meeting, or having a casual chat—will influence how close or distant you should be. Tune in to the other person's body language and adjust your approach as needed.

By being mindful of personal space, you can subtly enhance your interactions, making them more comfortable and effective for both you and the person you're engaging with.

Practice Makes Perfect

Like any other skill, reading and understanding body language takes practice. The more you observe and engage with others, the more attuned you'll become to the subtle cues that often go unnoticed. The good news? You don't have to be an expert from the get-go—just being aware and starting to pay attention to these signals is a huge first step.

Start Small. Begin by observing body language in everyday situations—whether it's at the office, during a coffee chat, or even while watching a TV show. Notice how people's gestures, posture, and facial expressions align (or don't) with what they're saying. As you become more aware, you'll start picking up on the nuances that add depth to conversations.

Reflect on Your Own Body Language. It's not just about reading others—your body language plays a big role in how you're perceived too. Practice being more conscious of your own gestures, posture, and expressions. Are you coming across as open and approachable? Are you unintentionally sending signals that might push people away? By tweaking your own nonverbal communication, you can make sure you're putting your best foot forward in every interaction.

Keep Learning. Remember, body language is a dynamic part of communication, and there's always more to learn. As you get more comfortable with the basics, challenge yourself to notice more subtle cues, like the way someone's eyes light up when they're genuinely interested or how their tone changes when they're nervous. The more you practice, the more natural it will become to "read the room" and respond accordingly.

Building Confidence. With practice, you'll find that your confidence in social situations grows. You'll start to trust your instincts more, knowing that you can pick up on the signals others are sending. This not only makes conversations smoother but also helps you connect on a deeper level, turning small talk into meaningful exchanges.

So, don't worry about getting it perfect right away—focus on being present, observing, and learning. With time, reading body language will become second nature, empowering you to navigate any social interaction with ease and confidence.

Recognizing Verbal Cues

Words are powerful, but they're only part of the story. How we say something can be just as important—if not more so—than the words we choose. Verbal cues are like the secret ingredients in a recipe, adding depth and flavor to our conversations. When you learn to pick up on these cues, you start to see beyond the surface of the words, gaining a clearer understanding of what someone is really trying to communicate.

Think about the last time you asked someone how they were doing, and they replied with a simple "fine." Depending on their tone, that one word could mean anything from "I'm great!" to "I'm barely holding it together." That's the magic of verbal cues—they can reveal the unspoken emotions, intentions, and thoughts that lie beneath the surface.

In this section, we're going to dive into the art of recognizing verbal cues, starting with one of the most telling indicators: tone and context. Understanding these subtle signals can transform your conversations, making them more meaningful and helping you connect on a deeper level.

Picking Up on Tone & Context

Ever notice how the same words can mean completely different things depending on how they're said? That's the power of tone and context at work. The tone of voice adds emotion and intent to our words, while the context gives those words their true meaning. Together, they can transform a simple statement into something much more complex.

Take the word "sure," for example. Said with a bright, upbeat tone, it might convey enthusiasm and agreement:

"Sure, I'd love to!" But with a flat or hesitant tone, it can quickly shift to something more reluctant or even dismissive: "Sure, I guess." The words haven't changed, but the meaning has—and that's the essence of tone and context.

To really connect with others, it's important to pay attention not just to what they're saying, but how they're saying it. Is their tone matching their words? Does it fit the context of the conversation? If there's a disconnect, that's a cue to dig deeper and find out what's really going on.

Context is the other half of the equation. What's the situation surrounding the conversation? Who's involved? What's the mood? All these factors influence how a message is delivered and received. A joke that's hilarious in one setting might fall flat—or worse, offend—in another. Understanding the context helps you interpret tone correctly and respond appropriately.

As a hiring manager conducting interviews, I always pay close attention to both tone and context—sometimes to the applicant's benefit, but not always. If their tone and words don't quite align, I make it a point to dig deeper into the subject. There have been times when a candidate explained a difficult situation to my satisfaction, and their tone revealed the truth behind their words. But there have also been instances where their tone didn't match up, and they kept dodging the truth, signaling that they had something to hide. Being strong in these skills has saved me from some serious hiring mishaps!

Practical Tips for Picking Up on Tone & Context:

- **Listen Beyond the Words:** Pay close attention to the tone of voice and how it aligns with the words being spoken. Are they enthusiastic, hesitant, sarcastic, or serious? Tone can completely alter the meaning of a phrase.

- **Consider the Situation:** Think about the context in which the conversation is happening. Is it a casual chat, a serious meeting, or a stressful situation? The context will often guide the tone and help you understand the underlying message.

- **Notice Any Discrepancies:** If someone's words don't match their tone, it's worth exploring further. For example, if they're saying they're "fine" but their tone is anything but, it might be an opportunity to offer support or ask a follow-up question.

- **Adjust Your Response:** Once you've picked up

on the tone and context, you can tailor your response to match. This shows that you're tuned in and engaged, making the conversation more meaningful for both parties.

By paying close attention to tone and context, you can unlock a deeper understanding of what's really being communicated. It's a skill that, with practice, becomes second nature, helping you navigate conversations with greater insight and confidence. But tone and context are just the beginning—there's more to verbal cues than meets the ear. Next, we'll dive into how emphasis and pauses can further reveal the nuances of what someone is really saying.

Listening for Emphasis and Pauses

When people talk, it's not just what they say that matters—it's also how they say it. The way someone emphasizes certain words or takes deliberate pauses can provide valuable insights into their thoughts and feelings. These subtle verbal cues can help you understand what's really important to them, what they might be uncertain about, or even what they're avoiding.

Emphasis: The Verbal Highlighter: Emphasis is like a verbal highlighter, drawing attention to specific words or ideas. When someone stresses a particular word or phrase, they're signaling that it's important. For example, saying "I really appreciate your help" emphasizes gratitude, while "I didn't agree with that decision" highlights disagreement. By tuning in to where someone places emphasis, you can gain a clearer understanding of their priorities and concerns.

Pauses: The Power of Silence: Pauses are just as telling as emphasis—maybe even more so. A well-placed pause can indicate hesitation, reflection, or the need for time to process thoughts. If someone pauses before answering a question, it might suggest they're carefully considering their response or that they're uncertain about what to say. On the other hand, a pause after a statement can invite further discussion or signal that they're expecting a reaction.

Reading Between the Lines: Emphasis and pauses are often used together to convey complex emotions or ideas. For instance, consider the difference between saying, "I think we should go with this plan" (emphasizing collaboration) and "I think we should go with this plan" (suggesting uncertainty). Similarly, a pause before the word "think" might indicate that the speaker is weighing their options. These subtle cues help you "read between the lines" and respond more thoughtfully.

Practical Tips for Listening for Emphasis and Pauses:

- **Tune In to Key Words:** Pay attention to the words or phrases someone emphasizes. These are often the key points they want to communicate, so respond in a way that acknowledges their importance.

- **Notice Pauses:** Be mindful of when and where someone pauses during a conversation. Are they pausing to reflect, or does it signal hesitation? Use these pauses as opportunities to ask follow-up questions or offer support.

- **Reflect Back:** When you notice emphasis or a significant pause, reflect it back in your response. For example, if someone says, "I really need help with this project," you might reply, "I can see that this project is really important to you. How can I assist?"

- **Practice Active Listening:** Active listening involves being fully present in the conversation and noticing not just the words but the nuances in how they're delivered. The more you practice, the better you'll become at picking up on these subtle verbal cues.

By paying attention to emphasis and pauses, you can unlock deeper layers of meaning in your conversations. These cues often reveal what's truly on someone's mind, helping you respond with greater empathy and understanding. Next, we'll explore how word choice can further inform you about a person's intentions and emotions.

Understanding Word Choice

Words are powerful, and the ones people choose often reveal more than they intend. While tone and emphasis add layers of meaning, the specific words someone uses can offer valuable insights into their thoughts, emotions, and intentions. By paying close attention to word choice, you can better understand not only what's being said but also what's left unsaid.

But it's not just about understanding others—your own word choice matters just as much. The words you select can shape how you're perceived, influence the direction of a conversation, and even affect the outcomes of your interactions. Being mindful of your word choice can help

you communicate more clearly, build stronger connections, and avoid misunderstandings.

Word Choice as a Window into Intent: The words
someone chooses can indicate how they feel about the topic at hand. For example, consider the difference between
someone saying, "I need to talk to you" versus "We should
chat." The first suggests urgency or seriousness, while the
latter feels more casual and open-ended. Word choice gives
you clues about the speaker's mindset and the nature of
the conversation that's about to unfold.

Formal vs. Informal Language: The level of formality
in language can also tell you a lot about the relationship
between the speakers and the situation. Formal language
often indicates professionalism, distance, or respect, while
informal language suggests familiarity, comfort, or even
intimacy. If someone switches from formal to informal
language (or vice versa) mid-conversation, it might signal a
shift in how they perceive the relationship or the conversation's direction.

Vague vs. Specific Language: People sometimes use
vague language to avoid commitment or confrontation.
Phrases like "maybe," "sort of," or "we'll see" can indicate hesitation, uncertainty, or a desire to keep things
open-ended. On the other hand, specific language, such
as "I'll get that to you by Friday" or "Let's meet at 10

a.m.," shows confidence, clarity, and a commitment to action. Recognizing these differences can help you navigate conversations more effectively, knowing when to push for specifics or when to give someone space.

Positive vs. Negative Framing: The way someone frames their statements—positively or negatively—can reveal a lot about their outlook or emotional state. For example, saying, "This project is challenging, but I'm learning a lot," frames the situation positively, focusing on growth and opportunity. On the other hand, "This project is overwhelming, and I don't know if I can handle it," carries a more negative, stressed tone. Picking up on these framings helps you understand the person's perspective and respond with the appropriate level of support or encouragement.

I live by this quote from T. Harv Eker: "*What you focus on expands*." That's one of the reasons why we worked on shifting your mindset from a negative focus to a positive one in an earlier chapter. Pay attention to the words you use until you've eliminated negative energy words from your language and replaced them with positive, empowering language. This one change can create a ripple effect of positivity in your life, transforming not just your conversations but your overall outlook.

Listening for Underlying Themes: Sometimes, the words people choose can hint at underlying themes or issues. If someone frequently mentions "stress," "pressure," or "overwhelm," even in unrelated contexts, it might indicate that these feelings are more prevalent in their life than they're explicitly stating. Recognizing these patterns can help you address concerns that the person might not feel comfortable bringing up directly.

Practical Tips for Understanding Word Choice:

- **Pay Attention to Repeated Words:** If someone keeps using the same word or phrase, it's likely significant. It can give you insight into what's weighing on their mind or what they value most.

- **Notice Shifts in Language:** A sudden change from formal to informal language, or from vague to specific, can signal a shift in the conversation. Use these cues to adjust your response accordingly.

- **Reflect Their Language Back:** Mirroring the key words or phrases that someone uses can help build rapport and show that you're tuned in to their message. For example, if they describe something as "exciting," you might respond with, "That does sound exciting—tell me more!"

- **Ask Clarifying Questions:** If someone's word choice is vague or unclear, don't be afraid to ask for more details. Phrases like "Can you elaborate on that?" or "What do you mean by that?" can help you get to the heart of the matter.

Understanding word choice is about listening with intention and curiosity. By paying close attention to the words people use, you can gain deeper insights into their thoughts, feelings, and motivations, making your conversations more meaningful and impactful.

Congratulations! You've just added another powerful tool to your social toolkit—the ability to read and respond to social cues with confidence and ease. Understanding body language, tone, context, and word choice might seem like a lot to juggle, but with practice, these skills will become second nature. You'll find yourself navigating conversations with a new level of insight, catching those subtle signals that used to fly under the radar.

Think of it like learning to play a musical instrument. At first, you're focused on each note, trying to get everything just right. But as you keep practicing, you start to play more naturally, letting the music flow. That's how it is with social cues. The more you pay attention and practice, the more you'll find yourself moving through conversations smoothly, building stronger connections, and leaving lasting impressions.

Remember, it's not about being perfect. Everyone has moments where they miss a cue or misinterpret a signal. The key is to stay curious, keep learning, and most importantly, enjoy the process. Social interactions are as much about connection as they are about communication, and by honing these skills, you're setting yourself up for richer, more meaningful relationships.

So go out there, listen with intent, observe with curiosity, and speak with purpose. Whether you're at a networking event, a casual gathering, or just catching up with a friend, you now have the tools to turn every interaction into an opportunity for genuine connection. And who knows? You might even find that reading social cues becomes one of your favorite parts of engaging with others.

Now, let's take these newfound skills and put them into practice—because the world is full of conversations just waiting to happen, and you're more than ready to dive in!

Reflections & Practice

HAVING COVERED LOTS OF ground decoding verbal and nonverbal patterns people show, let's outline a few ways to start cementing cue recognition skills through continual practice:

1. **Watch a video:** Study educational clips detailing positive/negative body language signals and facial expressions. Test your ability to notice and name the ones you see in the videos and those you observe in casual and business conversations out and about. What insights unfold?

2. **Catalog verbal cues:** Carry a small notepad while chatting with friends or family. Track concerns, worries, or emotional tones hinted at indirectly through their comments for more conscious responses. What undercurrents lie beneath the surface?

3. **Assess approach alignment:** Pause reflectively

after finishing up any meeting or event. Identify a few ways you could have adapted your communication style had you recognized verbal/nonverbal cues signaling something lacked optimal flow. Consider alternate responses for next time.

 Decoding social dynamics requires dedication, weaving perception, emotional intelligence, and behavioral adaptivity all simultaneously! But engaging experiences reward awareness widening. So, plunge boldly and expect a few faux pas to pave the way for growth to continue. Onward nomad to next discoveries about aligning language itself more thoughtfully given context.

After covering how to assess various social situations and adjust your small talk approach accordingly, there is still much more nuance to learn about adapting communication for deeper connections. In Chapter 10, we'll explore moving conversations smoothly from polite chatter to vulnerable sharing as trust and understanding build.

Chapter 9

Tailoring Communication Style to Situation

IT'S TIME TO TAKE those skills to the next level by mastering the art of adaptability. Whether you're chatting with a close friend, presenting to a boardroom, or resolving a conflict with a colleague, the way you convey your message can make all the difference. Tailoring your communication style to suit the situation is a skill that not only helps you connect more effectively with others but also enhances your ability to influence, inspire, and resolve issues. In this chapter, we'll explore how to apply everything you've learned so far, ensuring that you're always speaking the right language—no matter the context.

Understanding Your Audience

Communication isn't just about what you say—it's also about how your message is received. And that largely depends on who's on the other end of the conversation. Understanding your audience is the first step in tailoring your communication style to fit the situation. Whether you're speaking with a close friend, a colleague, or a potential client, recognizing their needs, expectations, and preferences can help you adjust your approach for maximum impact.

Who Are You Talking To?

The first thing to consider is who you're communicating with. Is it someone you know well or someone you're meeting for the first time? Are they a peer, a subordinate, or someone in a position of authority? Each of these factors will influence the tone, language, and level of formality you should use.

For example, in one of my past roles, I was responsible for presenting quarterly safety meetings to all the employees in our region. As I traveled from one location to the next, I quickly realized that my presentation couldn't be a one-size-fits-all approach. I needed to adjust my communication style depending on my audience—whether it was managers, office staff, or field workers. The language I used for the managers was more formal and strategic, focusing on leadership and compliance. For the office staff, I adopted a more collaborative tone, emphasizing teamwork and office safety. Meanwhile, when speaking to the field workers, I used straightforward, practical language that resonated with their hands-on experience. By tailoring my presentation to each group, I ensured that my message was well-received and that the content was relevant and engaging for everyone.

Adapting Language and Tone

Your audience's background, knowledge level, and expectations should guide your choice of language and tone. If you're speaking to someone well-versed in a particular subject, you can use industry-specific jargon or dive into complex details. However, if your audience is less familiar with the topic, it's important to simplify your language and avoid overwhelming them with too much information.

Tone is equally important. For instance, a casual, upbeat tone might be perfect for engaging a younger audience, while a more measured, professional tone could be better suited for a formal business setting. By tuning into what your audience needs and expects, you can create a more meaningful and effective exchange.

Considering Cultural and Social Norms

Different audiences may have different cultural or social norms that influence how they communicate and what they expect from others. Being aware of these differences can help you avoid misunderstandings and show respect for the other person's perspective. For example, in some cultures, direct eye contact is a sign of confidence, while in others, it might be considered disrespectful. Understanding these nuances allows you to tailor your approach in a way that aligns with your audience's values and expectations.

Reading the Room

Understanding your audience also means being able to "read the room." Are they engaged and interested, or do they seem distracted and disinterested? Picking up on these cues can help you adjust your approach on the fly, shifting the focus, changing the tone, or even altering the topic to better suit the mood.

By taking the time to understand your audience, you're not just speaking at them—you're speaking with them. This level of connection makes your communication more impactful, ensuring that your message resonates and leaves a lasting impression.

Assessing the Context

Understanding your audience is a crucial first step in effective communication, but it's only part of the equation. Equally important is assessing the context in which the communication takes place. The setting, purpose, and circumstances surrounding a conversation can drastically influence how your message is received. Just as you adapt your style to suit your audience, you also need to tailor it to fit the context.

The Role of Setting

The environment where a conversation happens plays a significant role in shaping the communication style you should adopt. A casual coffee chat with a colleague, for instance, allows for a more relaxed and informal tone, while a formal business meeting demands a more structured and professional approach. The setting often dictates the level of formality, the choice of words, and even the topics that are appropriate to discuss.

Purpose Drives Communication

Every conversation has a purpose, whether it's to inform, persuade, collaborate, or simply connect. Understanding the primary goal of the interaction helps you determine the most effective way to communicate. For example, if your goal is to persuade, you might choose to focus on benefits and outcomes, using compelling language and strong arguments. If the purpose is to inform, clarity and conciseness will be your guiding principles.

By aligning your communication style with the purpose of the conversation, you ensure that your message is not only heard but also understood and acted upon.

Timing is Everything

Context isn't just about where or why you're communicating—it's also about when. The timing of a conversation can greatly affect its outcome. For example, delivering important news at the end of a long, exhausting day might not be received as well as it would be in the morning when everyone is fresh and focused. Assessing the best time to have a conversation can be just as important as the words you choose to use.

Adjusting on the Fly

Just as with understanding your audience, being able to read the room and adapt to the context is key. Sometimes, the context of a conversation can shift unexpectedly. A casual chat might turn into a serious discussion, or a formal meeting might relax into a more open dialogue. Being attuned to these shifts allows you to adjust your communication style in real time, keeping the conversation on track and ensuring that your message remains effective.

In a previous position, I worked closely with a boss who embodied the perfect Southern gentleman—polite, composed, and always measured in his communication. Our conversations typically mirrored his style, focusing on pleasantries and respectful exchanges. However, there were times when my role required me to bring up tougher issues or take a stronger stance on certain actions we needed to discuss.

I quickly learned that to navigate these conversations effectively, I needed to preface them by signaling that this was going to be a tougher discussion. By giving him a heads-up, I allowed him to mentally prepare for a shift in tone and content, which helped him accept the stronger stance I needed to take. This small adjustment made our conversations more productive and ensured that even difficult topics were approached with the respect and understanding that matched his communication style.

Bringing It All Together

When you combine an understanding of your audience with a clear assessment of the context, you create a powerful foundation for effective communication. It's about more than just delivering a message—it's about delivering it in a way that resonates, engages, and achieves your desired outcome.

By assessing the context alongside understanding your audience, you're equipped to handle any communication scenario with confidence and finesse. This dynamic approach ensures that your message not only fits the situation but also leaves a lasting, positive impact.

Choosing the Right Medium

While there are countless ways to communicate—emails, texts, phone calls—nothing quite compares to the impact of face-to-face conversations. In-person interactions allow for richer communication, where body language, tone, and immediate feedback all play vital roles. When you can speak with someone directly, you can build stronger connections, gauge reactions in real time, and adjust your approach on the spot.

In this book, our focus is on mastering those in-person interactions where your presence and ability to read the room truly matter. While other mediums have their place, the skills you're developing here are all about making the most of face-to-face communication.

Reflecting and Adapting

Mastering the art of communication isn't just about learning new skills—it's also about continuously refining those skills through reflection and adaptation. After every key interaction, it's valuable to take a moment to reflect on what went well, what could have been better, and how you can improve in the future. This practice of reflection helps you become more self-aware and better equipped to adapt your communication style in different situations.

The Power of Reflection

After an important conversation or meeting, it's easy to move on to the next task without giving it a second thought. But taking just a few minutes to reflect can make a big difference in your ongoing development as a communicator. Ask yourself: Did I connect with my audience? Did I adjust my tone and language appropriately for the context? Was my message clear and well-received? By answering these questions, you gain insights that can help you improve your approach in future interactions.

Adapting Based on Feedback

Feedback—whether it's direct or indirect—provides another valuable opportunity for growth. If someone gives you feedback on your communication style, listen with an open mind. Even if the feedback is tough to hear, it's a chance to learn and adapt. Similarly, pay attention to nonverbal cues and the overall response to your communication. Did people seem engaged or disinterested? Did they ask questions or seem confused? These responses offer clues about how you might adjust your style next time.

Continuously Refining Your Approach

Effective communication is a dynamic skill that evolves over time. What works well in one situation might not work in another, and that's okay. The key is to keep refining your approach based on your experiences and what you've learned. As you continue to practice, you'll find that adapting your communication style becomes more intuitive, and you'll be better equipped to handle a wide range of situations with confidence.

Embracing Flexibility

Remember, flexibility is your greatest asset in communication. The more adaptable you are, the more effectively you can connect with others, no matter the context or audience. By reflecting on your interactions and making thoughtful adjustments, you'll continue to grow as a communicator, building stronger relationships and achieving greater success in both your personal and professional life.

As we bring this chapter to a close, it's clear that the ability to tailor your communication style to fit the situation is an invaluable skill. It's not just about mastering one way of interacting; it's about being versatile, flexible, and adaptable in your approach. Whether you're speaking with a friend, a colleague, or a potential client, the key to effective communication lies in your ability to adjust—shifting your tone, language, and even your demeanor to meet the needs of the moment.

This versatility in communication is like having a well-stocked toolbox. The more tools you have, the better equipped you are to handle any challenge that comes your way. You've learned how to understand your audience, assess the context, and reflect on your interactions—all of which are essential tools in your communication toolkit. However, true art lies in knowing when and how to use it, seamlessly transitioning from one style to another as the situation demands.

Remember, communication is not a rigid process; it's a dynamic exchange. By embracing the art of versatility, you become not just a participant in conversations but a master of them. You create connections that are not only effective but meaningful, fostering understanding, collaboration, and trust in every interaction.

So, as you move forward, take pride in your ability to adapt. Let your communication style be as varied and vibrant as the situations you encounter. With the tools and insights you've gained, you're well on your way to becoming a truly versatile communicator, ready to tackle any conversation with confidence and ease.

Reflections & Practice

LET'S TAKE SOME TIME to integrate the core concepts we just covered. Contemplating questions and translating insights into tangible action steps will exponentially accelerate your small talk metamorphosis.

So, find a quiet, comfortable place to ponder purposefully over the next half hour with a pen and journal handy. I encourage jotting down immediate reactions uncensored as they arise. We'll refine things into more formalized self-development plans later. For now, let your reflections flow freely!

1. What spoken or unspoken "rules" about small talk etiquette did your family or culture imprint growing up? Which still feels true or false for you today?

What specific guidelines or behaviors were emphasized in your household or community? Were certain topics deemed appropriate or inappropriate for casual conversations? Were you encouraged always to be polite and avoid controversial subjects?

2. What specific small-talk fears or failings keep you up at night? What "worst case scenarios" about casual conversation do you irrationally obsess over?

What aspects of small talk cause your anxiety? Is it the fear of running out of things to say, making a social faux pas, or being judged by others?

What "worst-case scenarios" about casual conversations do you obsess over irrationally? For example, do you worry about awkward silences, embarrassing statements, or offending someone unintentionally?

Which fears are based on past experiences, and which are purely speculative? Reflect on whether your fears have come true and how you handled those situations.

How do these fears affect your ability to engage in small talk? Consider both the short-term and long-term impacts on your social interactions and relationships.

3. When has social risk-taking paid off for you relationally? What happened when you stepped further out of your comfort zone interpersonally?

Here's one of my recent examples. When we moved to Puerto Rico, leaving our friends and family behind, we had to find friends and community on this beautiful island. It took us a couple of months to really get settled before loneliness for friends hit us. I joined some social groups online to get suggestions about our move, so I started watching those for some in-person social opportunities.

First, I saw an announcement about a group of guys gathering at a local pizza place with outdoor seating for cigars and conversations. I told Roger about it, so he attended and met several men. Some of those new friends then organized dinners at their homes and restaurants to connect as couples. Our local friend group had begun!

The second opportunity we quickly found was a local networking group called Uncommon Entrepreneurs, meeting at that same local pizza place. This was my first networking event on the island. The host greeted us at the sign-in table, and, learning we were new residents, he took us around, introducing us to other folks in our community.

I had grown so far in small talk and networking, but here I was, starting over with no friends. I was so proud of myself for willingly stepping out and visiting with friends who have become our island family.

It's your turn! Write out some successes you already see as you put yourself out there more and become more comfortable with networking and small talk.

4. Document additional mini-epiphanies, memoir-esque moments of truth, or snippets of wisdom from your distinct small talk expedition thus far. What aha's most resonated or surprised you?

I've realized that struggling with small talk is a universal experience. This book helped me see through the polished social masks we wear, revealing that others' outward confidence is often just as constructed as mine. This understanding has made me more compassionate toward others who might feel invisible and anxious. It's comforting to know that even celebrities and socially gifted friends have their moments when charm and humor don't come easily. We're all in this together, facing the same challenges beneath the surface. Dig deep to write a few of your own aha moments!

5. What lingering questions or skeptical spidey senses still itch around aspects of the book's core advice so far?

Air your doubts candidly without self-judgment. I don't really understand using humor for more comfortable small talk, except about myself, but others of you will embrace it as a tool you can use.

What universal insight or skillset gap do you think a bonus chapter might fill? Could we petition the publisher to address any conversational domains needing to be de-mystified in appendices?

6. Identify moments in past conversations where you could have gone deeper.

Rather than letting hindsight make us cringe when we recall talks that dead-ended awkwardly, why not mine memorably meaningful exchanges and near misses full of untapped potential?

For instance, chatting with my new neighbor while grabbing mail recently, we bonded quickly as flower lovers. But comments about pandemic isolation challenges lingered unexplored after initial sympathy laughs about kids causing quarantine chaos. We could have gone deeper, enriching our relationship as we do.

7. What past conversation moments come to mind for you where seizing subtle openings for empathy might have led to resonance?

List topics that interest you for deeper conversation.

Beyond biggies like spirituality, relationships, purpose, passions, or politics lies other rich repositories awaiting activated dialogue:

- Family traditions treasured carrying metaphysical meaning

- The perfect song, aroma, and film uniquely

transporting special headspaces

- Playful personality tests revealing "patronus" animals or moral motifs

- Lighthearted debates on ice cream flavor superiority rankings

- Favorite comeback stories or unsung local heroes deserving praise

8. What topics within your interests spark the most enthusiasm, elevating discourse deeper?

What are your passions? What subjects or activities make you feel genuinely excited and engaged? These include hobbies, professional interests, personal experiences, or intellectual pursuits. List a few that come to mind.

How can you introduce these topics into casual conversations naturally? What questions or statements can help you bridge the conversation toward these deeper subjects?

How can you balance sharing your enthusiasm with being approachable and inclusive? Reflect on ways to gauge the other person's interest and ensure the conversation remains two-way.

By exploring these prompts, you can better understand what drives your most engaging conversations and how to incorporate these elements into your interactions, fostering deeper and more fulfilling connections.

As our conversation matures, what greater heights can we scale together? How can we build upon the robust foundations established thus far? Join me as we discover new possibilities in the next chapter.

Chapter 10

Continuous Improvement

LET'S FINISH STRONG, FRIEND. Before we dive into the next leg of our journey towards mastering small talk, let's take a quick stroll down memory lane.

Remember that first chapter where I laid out my backstory, complete with all the social awkwardness? Back then, my entire identity was wrapped up in this "shy introvert" narrative, as if it were a fixed trait I was helplessly born with instead of a skill set I could develop.

I embraced that persona with gusto, letting it define me whenever professional events or new social situations triggered my anxiety. I clung to the edges of networking events, avoiding eye contact and sticking to the sidelines. Not exactly my best self!

But then came a series of wake-up calls—both personal and career milestones—that pushed me to step out of my comfort zone. I realized that if I wanted more out of life, I couldn't keep hiding behind that old narrative. No more playing small!

What motivated me? The desire for a richer life filled with social impact and meaningful achievements. To make that happen, I had to change my habits.

At first, it was all about baby steps—what I like to call "exposure therapy." I started initiating mini conversations with people I saw daily, slowly desensitizing myself and building up my chit-chat muscles. Those small steps began to add up, and before long, talking with strangers went from a nerve-wracking performance to something I started to enjoy.

We've covered a lot of ground together—unpacking psychological hangups, mastering foundational techniques, navigating specific situations, and making crucial mindset shifts. By now, you've hopefully got a solid arsenal of small talk skills ready to flex at your next networking event or social gathering.

But here's the thing: the best conversationalists don't stop at the basics. Once the surface skills are solid, that's when communication transforms from simple exchanges into an art form where unexpected wisdom is shared between open minds.

If you're ready to elevate your conversations from competent to truly memorable, Chapter 10 has plenty in store for you! No judgment if you're content with keeping things casually charming—there's value in that, too. But I've found that when you push the boundaries of small talk, a whole new universe of connection opens up.

This chapter is about continuously evolving how we intellectually and emotionally engage with others. It's about unlocking deeper layers of understanding and cultivating communities of trust where people feel safe enough to share their most profound thoughts.

Fair warning—it's all actionable content from here on out! We're talking about formalized plans to take your improved sociability to the next level. If you're excited by the idea of turning scattered skills into a structured system, then let's dive in! But no pressure—just making it this far already puts you ahead of the game.

Self Reflection

With your growth goals clarified, it's time to dig even deeper and assess your current conversational abilities—the foundation upon which any meaningful improvements can be built. I suggest taking some time to journal through the following reflection questions with openness and without judgment. The goal here is to quiet your inner critic and focus on gathering insightful baseline data that highlights areas for growth rather than reinforcing limiting self-perceptions.

- **What recurring remarks or listener reactions have hinted at areas where I could make adjustments to build stronger connections? Are there subtle cues suggesting room for refinement?**

- **When reflecting on recent conversations, how often did I truly listen versus talking over others or impatiently steering the conversation? Did the dialogue feel balanced, or was it dominated by my own thoughts and concerns?**

- **What facial expressions or body language cues might I have missed that signaled discomfort or disengagement from my conversation partner?**

- **Did I manage to steer the conversation back on track when it started drifting too far off course, or did I miss opportunities to explore shared curiosities more deeply?**

- **What universal insecurity or past experience**

might have triggered my tendency to hold back or hide socially, preferring the safety of being a wallflower?

Growing up, my family always told me not to "brag," which made me hesitant to share my true thoughts or passions beyond light, superficial conversations. Only recently have I started challenging the idea that genuine self-expression equals arrogance. This shift has been transformative, and now I'm much more confident in my conversations.

Developing Discussion Diagnostics

To keep my improvement efforts on track, I realized that occasional self-checks weren't enough. Relying solely on instincts can be tricky—our perceptions are often clouded by bias. So, I decided to introduce measurable metrics into my routine to quantify my progress in conversational skills.

Tracking tangible milestones has given me concrete evidence of growth. For instance, I monitor my weekly social engagements, count the number of new people I introduce myself to, and note new words I learn daily. Even small steps, when consistently tracked, can add up to significant progress over time. Using apps or digital tools to document my development has made it much easier to stay motivated and see how far I've come.

I suggest creating your own system to track conversational competency goals. Whether it's a personalized spreadsheet, a smart device dashboard, or even a simple journal, the key is to set up regular reminders to review your progress against your initial benchmarks. This way, you can clearly see your improvements and keep the momentum going. Here's a sample weekly schedule to get you started:

- **Monday:** Track the total time spent in conversations with strangers. Are you pushing yourself to engage more, even in brief exchanges?

- **Tuesday:** Record the number of new ice-breaker questions you've tested when talking to unfamiliar people. How are they working out? Are they sparking the conversations you want?

- **Wednesday:** Stand in front of a mirror and repeat your favorite innate qualities or talents aloud. How does it feel to own these traits? This helps build confidence and authenticity in your communication.

- **Thursday:** Take note of instances where you subtly corrected inauthentic mannerisms. Are you becoming more aware of when you're not being true to yourself in conversations?

- **Friday:** Journal the emotions that arise during social interactions and the insights you gain from each encounter. What patterns are you noticing? How are these experiences contributing to your growth?

By integrating these diagnostics into your routine, you'll have a clearer picture of your progress and areas that might need extra attention. The goal is to move beyond vague self-assessments and start seeing your conversational growth in real, measurable terms.

The Learning Launchpad

Developing strong conversational skills requires more than just reading about techniques—it involves active practice and reflection. To help you on this journey, consider the Learning Launchpad as your go-to method for turning theory into action. Here's how you can start applying what you've learned through targeted exercises and self-assessment.

Journaling as a Practice Tool

Imagine you're attending a small group session at a new
church, filled with unfamiliar faces. The leader asks everyone to introduce themselves by sharing their spiritual
journeys. As the spotlight moves toward you, panic sets
in. How might you navigate this tricky introduction with
grace? Try drafting a few personalized responses in your
journal. Once you've written them out, analyze your approach—what worked well, and what could be optimized
for next time?

Here's another prompt to consider: You're invited at
the last minute to a distant cousin's baby shower, and
the room is filled with family members chatting about
parenting and gossip. What engaging icebreaker questions
could you ask to sustain interesting dialogue throughout
the event? Write out your ideas and then review them.
Which talking points seem promising, and which might
fall flat? Fine-tune your phrasing to prepare conversational
scripts that feel natural and accessible when you're in the
moment.

Crafting Your Learning Process

Here's a streamlined approach to crafting your learning journey:

1. **Identify Your Lagging Skills:** Start by pinpointing the specific conversational scenarios that make you feel stuck or awkward. Maybe it's starting conversations, keeping them going, or exiting gracefully. Focus on one or two skills that have been challenging for you recently.

2. **Write Sample Scripts:** Draft sample conversations based on those tricky situations. Include both your predicted awkward responses and the ideal responses you wish you could deliver more naturally. Don't be afraid to get creative—this is your chance to explore different approaches.

3. **Review and Adjust:** Once you've written your sample conversations, review them critically. Does any phrasing feel off or unlikely to work in a real situation? Refine your responses until they sound like something you'd comfortably say.

4. **Practice Solo:** Rehearse your preferred responses out loud, even in front of a mirror if it helps.

The goal is to make these responses second nature through repetition in a safe, pressure-free environment.

5. **Test with Trusted Friends:** Try out your conversation scenarios with close friends who can give you honest feedback. Ask them how your responses flow and where you might improve. Keep tweaking until you feel confident.

6. **Apply in Real Interactions:** Armed with your well-practiced scripts, start incorporating them into real-world conversations. Be strategic but also flexible—allow your newfound confidence to guide you through interactions, bridging the gap between what used to feel difficult and your new, confident communication style.

Building Confidence Through Practice

The Learning Launchpad is all about turning your conversational goals into reality through structured practice. By identifying your weak spots, crafting and refining scripts, and practicing both alone and with friends, you'll gradually build the confidence and skills needed to excel in any social situation.

Remember, the key to success is consistency. The more you engage in these exercises, the more natural your conversational skills will become, helping you navigate even the most challenging scenarios with ease.

Seeking Feedback

Improvement doesn't happen in a vacuum. To truly enhance your conversational skills, it's essential to seek feedback from others. By getting an outside perspective, you can gain valuable insights into how you come across in conversations and identify areas where you might need to adjust your approach. Here's how to incorporate feedback into your learning process:

Ask Trusted Friends

One of the most reliable sources of feedback is your circle of trusted friends. These are the people who know you well, understand your communication style, and genuinely want to see you succeed. Don't be afraid to ask them for honest feedback about your conversational skills. Whether it's how you initiate conversations, keep them going, or wrap them up, your friends can provide you with candid insights that can help you grow.

- **How to Ask:** Be specific when seeking feedback. Instead of asking, "How did I do?" try asking, "Did I come across as confident in that conversation?" or "Was my response clear and engaging?" The more targeted your questions, the more useful the feedback you'll receive.

Roleplay New Approaches

Roleplaying is a powerful way to practice new conversational techniques in a low-stakes environment. By simulating real-life scenarios with a trusted friend or mentor, you can test out different approaches, receive immediate feedback, and refine your skills before applying them in actual conversations.

- **How to Roleplay:** Choose a specific scenario that you find challenging, such as introducing yourself at a networking event or handling a difficult conversation at work. Then, act out the scenario with your friend playing the other person. Afterward, discuss what worked well and what could be improved. Roleplaying allows you to experiment with different strategies in a supportive setting.

Review Recordings

If you can record your conversations—whether through video calls, voice memos, or other means—take advantage of it. Reviewing recordings of your interactions can provide you with an objective look at how you communicate. You can analyze your tone, pacing, body language, and the flow of the conversation, giving you concrete areas to focus on.

- **How to Review:** When watching or listening to a recording, pay attention to both your verbal and nonverbal communication. Are you speaking clearly and confidently? Are you making eye contact and using appropriate gestures? Take notes on what you did well and where you see room for improvement. This self-assessment can be incredibly eye-opening.

Observe Great Conversationalists

Sometimes, the best way to improve is by learning from those who excel in the areas where you want to grow.

Observing great conversationalists in action—whether they're public speakers, colleagues, or even characters in a movie—can provide valuable lessons in effective communication.

- **How to Observe:** Take note of how skilled conversationalists navigate different types of interactions. How do they start conversations? How do they keep the dialogue engaging? What techniques do they use to build rapport and connect with others? By analyzing their strategies, you can adopt some of their best practices and adapt them to your own style.

Learning from the Best

You don't need to reinvent the wheel when there are so many mentors with valuable life lessons around you. Dive into podcasts by influencers discussing topics that interest you.

Reading a best-selling author's book, like mine, can help you spot the mistakes you're making in your conversations. Follow my tips to unlock easier and more effective communication!

Here's an example of how I applied trusted feedback to improve my conversational skills:

At networking events, I used to answer questions from others but never asked anything in return. This often led to awkward silences, waiting for someone else to pick up the conversation.

My husband reminded me that everyone loves talking about themselves, so he encouraged me to follow my answers with a question. Earlier in this book, I listed some of these questions, which made conversations much easier.

Initially, I felt surprised and a bit embarrassed by the critique, but I appreciated Roger's honesty and saw the truth in his feedback. Once conversations started, I was better equipped to keep them going and build deeper relationships.

Roger agreed to help me practice keeping the conversation flowing. We set guidelines like giving thorough answers instead of just a few words followed by a question. With practice, I found a good balance in my answers and questions.

We role-played different conversational scenarios, and I learned to share more about myself while always seeking to know more about others. I also learned to shift the conversation naturally to help the relationship grow.

Learning new habits was challenging at first, but the more we practiced, the more mindful I became of my role in guiding the conversation. My listening skills improved significantly thanks to Roger's help and willingness to change my approach to small talk.

Practicing Regularly

Like any skill, smooth small talk improves through regular repetition, gradually rewiring those once-reluctant reflexes. What initially triggered tension can start to flow with ease, all thanks to the power of committed consistency. Over time, daily practice compounds into newfound confidence and comfort in conversations.

I still vividly recall the days when I would hang back at networking events, hoping a familiar face would swoop in and save me from an awkward exchange. But after months of intentional practice—turning responses into muscle memory rather than a mental workout—public interactions became surprisingly enjoyable!

What helped me most? Setting mini-goals and creating micro-adventures that nudged me, a nervous novice, toward becoming a more confident conversationalist. Here are some of my handy habit hacks that exponentially boosted my casual chat abilities:

Daily Quick-Win Challenges

- **Greet three strangers daily** with friendly questions to spark conversations.

- **Rekindle camaraderie** by phoning a forgotten friend for a caring catch-up.

- **Craft two unique icebreaker jokes** to try at your next social gathering.

- **Roleplay introducing yourself smoothly** three times in front of a mirror or camera.

Conversation Sparks Schedule

I designated specific diary slots on certain days to strengthen my sociability circuits. Just as scheduling work deadlines or exercise routines builds accountability, consistently blocking time to face conversational fears helps ensure steady improvement.

Here's how I structured my regular rapport regimen:

- **Wednesday** - (Chat Roulette): I use uplifting greetings and icebreaker questions to connect with others during events like a women's coffee meeting or a Chamber of Commerce luncheon. These interactions plant seeds for new friendships, with something new sprouting every week.

- **Friday** - (Recording Review Day): I review video recordings to identify verbal and nonverbal cues, learning from both successes and missteps. This helps me grow my skills without the pressure of real-time interaction.

- **Sunday** - (Soulful Storytelling Practice): I write mini-memoirs of the week's social joys and successes. Where appropriate, I share these stories on social media to express gratitude for new connections. Reflecting on how far I've come reinforces my progress.

Quotes Sparking Small Talk Action

I bookmark motivational mantras that inspire me to master previously daunting social skills. When my motiva-

tion dips, these rallying cries help me refocus and push
through:

- *"Great things never came from within our comfort zones."* This quote propels me beyond initial trepidation, transforming overwhelming social scenarios into opportunities for growth. (Attributed to various sources but widely recognized
  as an anonymous saying.)

- *"Every master was once a beginner."* This reminder consoles me during awkward moments.
  Each stumble is proof that I'm pushing beyond
  the barriers that limit others who shy away from
  the risks required for growth. (Attributed to
  Robin S. Sharma.)

As you read books and gather inspiration, jot down
quotes that resonate with you. These mantras can keep
you motivated on your journey toward better communication.

On Habit-Forming

Dedication and gradual effort are the keys to improvement—not illusions of quick success. Persistently forming
new habits brings exponential returns. Over time, a natur-

al ease in conversation will replace the old reluctance that once held you back.

If you're hesitant to share stories with strangers or reconnect with old friends, don't worry! Consistent practice helped me overcome my own fears, bit by bit. My confidence grew, and now I navigate conversations with much greater ease. You can achieve this too, taking small, brave steps to build your social skills, despite any past shyness.

Keep pushing forward and unleash your dynamic personality with patience. Cultivating conversational courage, even when fear tries to hold you back, is invaluable. Ignore those timid inner voices, because a world of friendship and deeper connections is waiting just beyond your comfort zone. Celebrate the victories that were once out of reach due to hesitation. These hard-won achievements will lead to richer, more effortless dialogues.

Well, friend, look at us now! We've come a long way from those early days of awkward small talk and sweaty palms, haven't we? This chapter was all about taking everything we've learned and turning it into a solid, actionable plan for continuous improvement. But here's the kicker—this journey doesn't end here. Nope, we're just getting started!

Think of your conversational skills like a plant—you've got to keep watering it, giving it some sunlight, and maybe even talking to it a little (hey, it can't hurt!). The more you nurture your abilities, the stronger and more natural they'll become. Before you know it, you'll be the one people look to for how to handle a room, spark a conversation, or keep the dialogue flowing with ease.

Remember, it's not about being perfect. It's about showing up, trying new things, and not being afraid to stumble a little along the way. Every conversation is a chance to grow, to learn something new, and to connect with someone in a meaningful way. And that's what makes this whole process so exciting!

So, keep setting those mini-goals, keep practicing those quick wins, and don't forget to celebrate every victory—no matter how small. You're building something incredible here, and the best part is, it's all uniquely yours. Your voice, your style, your way of connecting with the world.

And when those old doubts start creeping in, just remember: You've got this. You've come this far, and there's no stopping you now. Keep pushing, keep growing, and keep having fun with it. After all, what's life without a little adventure?

Now, go out there and show the world what you're made of—one conversation at a time.

Reflections & Practice

MASTERING SMOOTH SMALL TALK means continual reflection & practice strengthening skills learned while addressing lagging spots. Let's outline some ways of translating insights recently uncovered into action today.

1. Reflect on recent conversations and identify strengths and areas for improvement.

I now habitually replay recent chats, no longer to overthink them like I used to, but now to identify what worked wonderfully or wavered weirdly in my approaches. Tracking positives to repeat and noting areas for improvement helps me adjust my style for future conversations.

For example, suppose my silly icebreaker joke was reciprocated humorously by an intimidating industry expert at last week's seminar. In that case, I'll remember that successful one-liner for future events with similarly esteemed colleagues. I can build on my successes and continually refine my conversational skills. Or maybe I noticed myself dominating dialogue with my cousin last brunch. My meandering monologues with minimal questions hint at where I need refinement to balance relational airspace at my next gathering with relatives. Trying to ask more follow-up questions comes next.

See how recognizing little wins and lagging spots post-interactions guides adept skills adjusted ongoing?

You can try it at the next event! Briefly journal what social approaches worked wonderfully with some folks while limitations still lurked with others. Then, make notes on how to improve before the next conversation based on review!

2. Ask friends or colleagues for feedback on your small talk skills

While self-assessment stands invaluable for pattern awareness, outside opinions also provide objective observations through unbiased lenses unavailable to us individually.

So, I suggest soliciting candid feedback from a few trusted friends about your communication style. Are any behaviors being unconsciously exhibited that limit connection? Their kind revelations shed light on blind spots to improve angles you likely haven't acknowledged yet walking solo.

Specifically request advice on:

• Your listening skills

- Reciprocity balance

- Warmth making others feel safe

- Quality of your questions

3. Set goals for practicing small talk regularly and track your progress.

Committing development intentions to writing weekly creates accountability and motivation for making progress. Note incremental improvements in conversational competence as consistency compounds.

For example, perhaps the initial goal is chatting with 1 stranger daily. But each week you push further:

- Week 1: Start small talk with 1 stranger

- Week 2: Start small talk with 3 strangers

- Week 3: Start small talk with 5 strangers

- Week 4: Start talks with 5 strangers and get 2 contacts

Having metrics plotted to praise micro wins builds confidence and fuels bigger conversational dreams destined through dedication.

I know it feels easier said than done by my friends. However, patient practice strengthens skills once shaky when interacting with strangers, resulting in eventual excellence in exchanging dialogue fluidly. We speak souls seamlessly through willingness walking relational edges wisely week on week.

In closing, improving any skill takes honest self-assessment, soliciting outside perspectives, and consistently dedicated practice to strengthen areas that are still progressing. We uncovered reflection habits evaluating conversational successes and limitations for correction going forward. We explored seeking input from trusted colleagues offering objective feedback on related approaches landing limiting for listeners, perhaps. We also outlined practical methods for tracking measurable gains through quantifiable goals, celebratory wins, and motivation compounding.

Can life-changing professional opportunities or income levels be consistent with ideas shared in previous chapters? Could our casual chatting comfort with strangers pave access previously out-of-reach at times?

I'm thrilled to witness first-hand the overflow derived from taking terrifying small talk risks. But you need not take just my word for it. Peer-reviewed research confirms positive correlations to everything I've shared. Move with

me to Chapter 11, where we share the long-term benefits
of good small talk.

Chapter 11

The Long-Term Benefits of Good Small Talk

WHEN I FIRST STARTED working on my small talk skills, my primary goal was simple: ease the awkwardness and anxiety that often accompany unfamiliar social situations and obligatory conversations. The idea of engaging in charming chit-chat felt unnatural and meeting new people outside my core group of friends seemed downright daunting.

However, after months of courageously developing my social skills through consistent practice, I began to understand why seasoned sages emphasize the importance of stepping out of your comfort zone and staying open to learning. Mastering the art of banter offers benefits far beyond merely surviving a dinner party or office mixer without dread.

In fact, peer-reviewed research strongly supports the positive impact of good conversational skills on various aspects of life, including health, career, and relationships. Studies show that people who connect with others tend to have lower mortality rates, higher income, greater leadership potential, and more fulfilling family and community lives. The rewards of good communication are far greater than we often realize.

Research by psychologist Gillian Sandstrom highlights that even casual interactions with strangers and acquaintances can significantly enhance our health, happiness, and well-being. Small talk can act as a bridge to deeper understanding and help us form connections with people we might initially think we have nothing in common with.

Kyle Kellams, a news director and radio host, points out that small talk is a gift we give each other, sometimes leading to meaningful connections. Studies also suggest that people are generally happier when conversing, even if it's just small talk with strangers on a plane, subway, or bus.

So, the next time you find yourself entering a social situation, remember that a simple chat can open doors to new opportunities and unexpectedly enrich your life.

Building Stronger Relationships

Building a robust professional or social network can have a profound impact on your life, but initiating conversations often feels daunting. This is where the power of genuine, friendly small talk comes into play. Instead of viewing interactions as purely transactional, focusing on personal connections can establish strong, mutually beneficial relationships.

Mastering the art of small talk lays the foundation for meaningful connections. When conversations are authentic and sincere, people are more likely to respond positively, fostering trust and collaboration. Over time, these connections can lead to new opportunities—both personally and professionally—enriching your overall quality of life.

Small talk isn't just about filling awkward silences; it's about finding common ground and showing genuine interest in others. Whether it's a casual chat at a networking event, a brief exchange with a colleague, or a friendly conversation with a stranger, each interaction holds the potential to open doors and leave lasting impressions.

The ability to engage in effective small talk can transform obligatory interactions into enjoyable experiences, paving the way for deeper relationships and exciting opportunities for growth and collaboration. So, the next time you find yourself in a social or professional setting, remember small talk isn't just small—it's the first step in building bridges that can lead to meaningful, lasting relationships.

Enhancing Personal Relationships

While small talk is often associated with networking and professional settings, its impact on personal relationships is just as significant. In fact, the ability to engage in meaningful small talk can be the glue that strengthens and deepens the bonds with the people closest to you.

Strengthening Everyday Connections: In our day-to-day lives, small talk serves as a way to maintain and nurture the connections we have with our family, friends, and partners. Those seemingly insignificant chats about how the day went, what's for dinner, or even the weather help to keep the lines of communication open. These small moments build a foundation of trust and understanding, creating a sense of closeness that's essential for any healthy relationship.

By regularly engaging in small talk with those you care about, you show that you're interested in their lives and invested in the relationship. It's not just about the words exchanged but the emotional connection that comes from being present, listening, and sharing your thoughts and feelings in return.

Deepening Emotional Bonds: Small talk also plays a key role in deepening emotional bonds. When you take the time to engage in light conversation, you create opportunities for more meaningful discussions to arise naturally. A simple question like "How was your day?" can lead to a deeper conversation about challenges, joys, or important decisions. Over time, these interactions help to foster a deeper understanding of each other's needs, values, and emotions.

In romantic relationships, small talk can be especially powerful. Regular, light-hearted conversations help maintain a sense of intimacy and keep the relationship vibrant. Whether it's sharing a laugh about something funny that happened during the day or reminiscing about a favorite memory, these moments of connection can enhance the overall happiness and satisfaction in the relationship.

Bridging Gaps and Resolving Conflicts: Small talk can also serve as a bridge during times of tension or conflict. When emotions are running high, engaging in neutral, light conversation can help to diffuse the situation and create a space for more constructive dialogue. It allows both parties to ease into a conversation without immediately diving into the tough stuff, making it easier to approach the issue with a calm and open mindset.

Moreover, small talk can help keep the relationship steady even when life gets busy or stressful. By maintaining regular, light communication, you ensure that the relationship stays connected, even when there's little time for in-depth discussions.

Creating Lasting Memories: Finally, small talk is often where some of the most cherished memories are made. Those spontaneous, off-the-cuff conversations that happen over breakfast, during a walk, or while doing chores together are the moments that often stick with us the longest. They create a sense of shared experience and joy, contributing to the overall richness of the relationship.

In essence, small talk is a powerful tool for enhancing personal relationships. It helps to maintain connections, deepen emotional bonds, bridge gaps during conflicts, and create lasting memories. By embracing the art of small talk in your personal life, you're investing in the quality and longevity of your most important relationships.

Dream Boldly Together

Explore exciting bucket list adventures that bring zest and adventure back into your long-term relationships. Support each other as you step out of your comfort zones, embracing lives aligned with your deepest passions and dreams.

Nurturing intimate relationships over the long haul means carving out consistent time for authentic sharing beyond the daily grind. Prioritize soulful conversations that range from healing past traumas to daring dreams about the future. These meaningful exchanges water the relational soil, yielding precious fruits of trust and connection.

Show up genuinely, again and again, creating a safe space where both partners can be seen, heard, and held through laughter, listening, or tears. This consistent authenticity unlocks the gates to a stronger bond, ready to write the next beautiful chapter together joyfully.

As we traveled and cruised, Roger and I started dreaming of living on a Caribbean island in the future. We dreamed vividly, even planning the work we'd be doing there, our friends joining us, and our island lifestyle. Over the years, I included a picture of the view from our island home on my vision board each year. Today, that view is mine! I don't believe we would be here if we hadn't dreamed it and spoken of it as though we were already living it.

The friends who dreamed with us never embraced the dream outside of our times cruising together, so none of them are living this lifestyle. My brother, however, shared his dream lifestyle with me a few years back when we were both working on growing our businesses. He kept the dream front and center over the years, and his dream lifestyle is now almost exactly as he described it to me.

Investing in our relationships and dreaming together creates meaningful, lasting bonds that enrich our lives and help us achieve our aspirations.

Creating Opportunities

Small talk may seem like a minor part of daily life, but its potential to open doors and create new opportunities is immense—especially in the professional world. Whether you're looking to advance in your career, build stronger networks, or simply stay visible in your industry, mastering the art of small talk can be a game-changer.

Professional Advancement

In my experience as an HR manager, I've seen countless employees with the technical skills to move up the corporate ladder but lacking the social finesse to close the deal. On the flip side, I've also encountered individuals whose overconfidence in social settings caused them to miss the mark in conversations with coworkers and managers. The key to professional advancement lies in finding the right balance—using small talk as a tool to connect authentically with others while staying attuned to the nuances of each interaction.

If you're aiming for a promotion or a career shift, now is the time to combine your business acumen with your social skills. Opportunities to advance may not always be immediately available, but by honing your small talk abilities, making genuine connections, and deepening important relationships, you position yourself to seize those opportunities when they do arise.

And who says you can't climb the career ladder through strategic rapport-building? Don't shy away from small talk, even with executives, during those brief elevator rides. You never know what creative connections might form through a mix of curiosity, care, and a bit of courage. Make the most of those short moments to build a sense of community with higher-ups and watch how these efforts can open doors to significant career opportunities.

Building Relationships and Networking

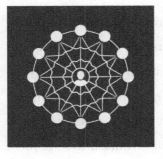 Small talk is the gateway to forming meaningful relationships with colleagues, superiors, and industry peers. These casual conversations help break the ice and lay the foundation for more profound professional connec-tions. Imagine attending a corporate event where you don't know anyone—initiating small talk about a recent industry development or even the weather can lead to en-gaging conversations and help you connect with influen-tial figures in your field.

For instance, I once struck up a conversation with a senior manager at a networking event about our mutual interest in hiring trends. What started as a simple exchange led to a deeper discussion about potential collaborations, eventually opening doors for a new project that signif-icantly boosted my career. These kinds of connections, initiated through small talk, can lead to substantial pro-fessional opportunities.

Building connections with industry peers can open doors to exciting new opportunities that you never knew existed. These are people working on similar projects, so you already have something in common. Start the conversation, and you never know which connection will lead to your next opportunity.

Enhancing Visibility and Recognition

Regular small talk can also increase your visibility in the workplace. Engaging in brief, friendly interactions makes you more recognizable and approachable, leading to greater collaboration and career advancement opportunities. By regularly greeting and having short conversations with your company's leadership, you stay on their radar, making it more likely for them to consider you for promotions or key projects.

I made it a habit to chat with my boss briefly each morning about non-work-related topics like weekend plans or sports. This helped build rapport, and when a leadership position opened up, I was among the first to be considered because I was already a familiar and trusted presence. These small, consistent interactions can significantly impact your career trajectory.

Building a Positive Workplace Reputation

Engaging in small talk can help you build a positive reputation at work. Being seen as friendly, approachable, and communicative makes you likable—an invaluable trait in team settings and collaborative environments. Consistently engaging in small talk with coworkers can help you build a reputation as a team player and a positive influence in the office. This can be beneficial when team leaders are looking for someone to head new initiatives.

Understanding and adapting to different communication styles is crucial in a diverse work environment. People have unique ways of expressing themselves, and recognizing these differences can improve your interactions and reduce misunderstandings.

For example, my husband prefers concise communication, especially when discussing problems—he expects solutions to be presented alongside the issues. Our accountant, on the other hand, asks detailed questions to fully understand our goals before offering advice. By adapting my communication style to match each individual, I built a reputation as someone approachable and easy to work with, which eventually led to more invitations to participate in key projects and a promotion to a stronger leadership position.

Creating Opportunities for Mentorship

Small talk can also pave the way for mentorship opportunities. Engaging in casual conversations with more experienced colleagues can open doors to informal mentoring relationships that guide and support your career growth. A casual conversation about a challenging project could lead to a senior colleague offering advice or becoming a mentor, helping you navigate your career path more effectively.

For instance, I once joined an online women's group, looking to make more connections. After a few weeks of posting in that group, the leader made a point to meet me in person when she noticed we were in the same place. From this connection, we began meeting regularly, eventually forming a mastermind group of women who supported each other in achieving our goals. These mentorships often start with simple, casual interactions that blossom into something much more significant.

Gaining Insights and Information

Small talk can provide valuable insights and information about your industry, company, or specific projects. These casual conversations can keep you informed and ahead of the curve. For example, through casual conversations during breaks, I learned about an upcoming project that perfectly matched my skills. This information allowed me to prepare and express my interest in the project early, ultimately leading to my involvement and success in the initiative.

Patience While Practicing

Professional opportunities don't always appear on our timeline, but that doesn't mean they won't come. I once interviewed for an executive position that seemed perfect for my qualifications. When I didn't get the job, I was disappointed but continued to serve well in my current role. A year later, the company reached out to offer me the position, which had become available again. By staying patient and prepared, I was ready when the opportunity finally came.

Enhancing Emotional Intelligence

Small talk isn't just about making conversation—it's also a powerful tool for enhancing your emotional intelligence (EQ). Emotional intelligence is the ability to understand, manage, and effectively express your own feelings, as well as the ability to engage and navigate the emotions of others. By mastering small talk, you can develop greater empathy, improve your social awareness, and strengthen your ability to connect with others on a deeper level.

One of the key components of emotional intelligence is empathy—the ability to put yourself in someone else's shoes and understand their perspective. Small talk, when done right, gives you the chance to practice this skill regularly. By paying close attention to the words, tone, and body language of the person you're speaking with, you can pick up on subtle emotional cues and respond in a way that shows you truly understand and care.

For example, a simple conversation about how someone's day is going can reveal a lot about their current emotional state. If they mention they're feeling overwhelmed at work, responding with empathy—acknowledging their stress and offering a supportive word—can go a long way in building trust and rapport. These small interactions help you develop a deeper understanding of the people around you, which is a cornerstone of strong emotional intelligence.

Small talk also enhances your social awareness, another critical aspect of emotional intelligence. Engaging in light conversation requires you to be present and attentive, reading the room and adjusting your approach based on the dynamics at play. Whether it's sensing when someone is ready to move on from a topic or recognizing when they need a bit more encouragement to open up, small talk helps you tune in to the social cues that guide effective communication.

Moreover, small talk gives you the opportunity to manage your own emotions in real time. If you're feeling nervous or uncertain in a social situation, practicing small talk can help you stay calm and focused. As you become more comfortable in these interactions, you'll find it easier to regulate your emotions and maintain a positive, confident demeanor.

In short, the practice of small talk is a valuable exercise in emotional intelligence. It sharpens your ability to empathize with others, boosts your social awareness, and helps you manage your own emotions with greater ease. Over time, these skills will not only make you a better conversationalist but also a more emotionally intelligent individual, capable of building stronger, more meaningful connections with those around you.

Confidence and Social Skills: The Game Changers

By now, you've likely realized that practicing small talk isn't just about getting better at conversation—it's about building a foundation of confidence and social skills that can truly change the game for you in all aspects of life.

Confidence: Your Secret Weapon: Confidence isn't just about feeling good in the moment; it's a powerful tool that can transform the way you approach every situation. When you're confident in your conversational abilities, you're more likely to step up, whether it's introducing yourself in a new environment, sharing your ideas boldly, or simply engaging with someone new. This self-assurance doesn't just help you start conversations—it empowers you to seize opportunities that might have once seemed out of reach.

Social Skills: The Key to Connection: Enhanced social skills give you the ability to connect with others on a deeper level, turning potentially awkward encounters into opportunities for meaningful interaction. Whether you're navigating a family reunion, a business event, or a casual get-together, strong social skills enable you to engage naturally, read the room effectively, and respond to social cues with ease.

Expanding Your Influence: With increased confidence and sharpened social skills, you'll find that your influence extends beyond just conversations. You'll notice that interactions, whether in your personal or professional life, become more productive and fulfilling. People are drawn to those who exude confidence and handle social situations with grace, which can lead to a wealth of new opportunities, from career advancements to deeper personal connections.

In essence, the confidence and social skills you've honed through small talk practice are more than just conversation tools—they're catalysts for broader success and deeper fulfillment in life. So, embrace these newfound strengths and let them guide you to new heights, both socially and professionally.

Fostering a Sense of Belonging

At its core, small talk is more than just a social skill—it's a gateway to fostering a genuine sense of belonging. When you engage in small talk, you're not just exchanging words; you're building connections that can make you and those around you feel truly included and valued.

This reminds me of the old sitcom Cheers, with its iconic theme song, written by Gary Portnoy and Judy Hart:

Sometimes you wanna go
Where everybody knows your name
And they're always glad you came
You wanna be where you can see
Our troubles are all the same
You wanna be where everybody knows your name.

There are certain people I've met along my journey where, from the first conversation, I just knew—I've found my people. We all long for that kind of genuine connection, and it only happens when we take the risk to chat with others as we walk our paths.

Creating Inclusive Spaces: One of the most powerful aspects of small talk is its ability to create inclusive environments. Whether you're at a community event, a work function, or a casual get-together, small talk helps break down barriers and invites others to participate in the conversation. By initiating or engaging in these light exchanges, you're sending a signal that everyone is welcome and that their presence is valued.

This inclusivity is vital, especially in larger groups where it's easy for some people to feel overlooked or out of place. A simple "How's your day going?" or "What do you think of this event?" can draw someone into the fold, making them feel like a part of the group rather than an outsider. These small gestures of connection can go a long way in creating a welcoming atmosphere where everyone feels they belong.

Building Community: Over time, consistent small talk can help you build a sense of community, whether it's within your neighborhood, workplace, or social circle. The more you engage with others through casual conversation, the more you strengthen the bonds that hold these communities together. Regularly chatting with neighbors, coworkers, or fellow members of a club or group fosters a network of support and shared experiences.

These small, everyday interactions lay the groundwork for deeper relationships and a more connected community. When people feel connected, they're more likely to support each other, collaborate, and contribute to the group's well-being. In this way, small talk becomes a powerful tool for cultivating a sense of unity and togetherness.

Enhancing Personal Fulfillment: Feeling like you belong isn't just good for your social life—it's also crucial for your personal well-being. When you regularly engage in small talk and build connections, you're more likely to feel anchored in your relationships and environment. This sense of belonging contributes to your overall happiness, reduces feelings of loneliness, and can even improve your mental health.

Moreover, knowing that you have a network of people who appreciate and value your presence boosts your self-esteem and confidence. It's a reminder that you're part of something larger than yourself, which can be incredibly fulfilling.

In essence, small talk is much more than idle chatter; it's a powerful means of fostering a sense of belonging. By engaging in these seemingly simple conversations, you're creating spaces where people feel seen, heard, and valued. And in return, you strengthen your own sense of connection and community, making the world around you a little bit more welcoming.

Longevity and Quality of Life

It might surprise you to learn that the benefits of small talk extend far beyond social circles and professional networks. In fact, engaging in regular conversations—no matter how casual—can have a profound impact on your longevity and overall quality of life. The simple act of connecting with others is deeply intertwined with both mental and physical well-being.

The Health Benefits of Social Interaction: Numerous studies have shown that strong social connections are linked to a longer, healthier life. Regular social interaction helps reduce stress, lowers the risk of depression, and even boosts your immune system. Small talk, as light and inconsequential as it may seem, plays a vital role in maintaining these connections. Every brief exchange—whether it's with a neighbor, a coworker, or a stranger at the coffee shop—helps to keep loneliness at bay and fosters a sense of belonging that's essential for well-being.

People who engage in frequent social interactions tend to be happier and more satisfied with their lives. This is because these interactions provide emotional support, stimulate the mind, and create a buffer against the stresses of daily life. When you make small talk a regular habit, you're essentially investing in your long-term health.

Mental Sharpness and Emotional Resilience: Engaging in small talk also helps keep your mind sharp. Conversations require you to think on your feet, respond to cues, and engage in a dynamic exchange of ideas. This mental stimulation is crucial as we age, helping to preserve cognitive function and keep our minds active. The more we converse, the more we exercise our brains, which can contribute to better mental health over the long haul.

Furthermore, the emotional resilience gained through regular social interaction cannot be understated. Small talk helps build relationships that offer emotional support during tough times. Knowing that you have a network of people you can talk to, even casually, creates a sense of security and can significantly reduce feelings of isolation.

A Happier, More Connected Life: Ultimately, small talk contributes to a happier, more connected life. The simple act of saying hello, asking someone how their day is going, or sharing a lighthearted joke can have a ripple effect, lifting your mood and the mood of those around you. These small moments of connection accumulate, creating a rich tapestry of relationships that enhance your life in countless ways.

By embracing small talk as a regular practice, you're not just improving your social skills—you're actively contributing to your health, happiness, and longevity. It's a simple yet powerful way to enrich your life and the lives of those you interact with, making each day a little brighter and a lot more meaningful.

The Ripple Effect

As we've journeyed through the many facets of small talk, it's clear that the impact of these seemingly simple interactions is far-reaching. The ripple effect of good small talk extends beyond the immediate moment, influencing various aspects of our lives in profound ways.

Starting with a Single Conversation: Every conversation you have, no matter how brief, has the potential to create a ripple effect. What begins as a casual chat can evolve into a deeper connection, opening doors to new opportunities, friendships, and collaborations. These connections, in turn, can lead to further interactions and relationships, expanding your social and professional network in ways you might never have anticipated.

Transforming Social Dynamics: The positive energy you bring to a conversation doesn't just benefit you—it affects everyone involved. When you engage in small talk with genuine interest and warmth, you set the tone for others to feel comfortable and included. This can transform the social dynamics of any setting, creating an environment where people are more open, collaborative, and supportive.

Enriching Your Life and Others: The ripple effect of small talk isn't just about creating new opportunities for yourself; it's also about enriching the lives of those around you. A friendly exchange can brighten someone's day, provide much-needed encouragement, or simply make them feel seen and heard. These small moments of connection contribute to a greater sense of community and belonging, making the world a little bit better with each interaction.

A Legacy of Connection: As you continue to practice and refine your small talk skills, remember that you're creating a legacy of connection. The relationships you build, the opportunities you seize, and the positive energy you spread through conversation will have lasting impacts—both for you and for those you interact with. The ripple effect of your efforts will continue to expand, touching lives in ways you may never fully realize.

In the end, good small talk isn't just about making conversation—it's about making a difference. It's about using your words and your presence to create waves of positive change, one conversation at a time. So keep talking, keep connecting, and watch as the ripples of your efforts spread far and wide, enriching your life and the lives of others in ways that truly matter.

Reflections & Practice

BEYOND NEXT WEEK'S PARTIES or professional mixer events, pausing periodically to assess communication competency's cascading fruits long-term is equally important to stay focused on continual improvement. Here are impactful self-inventories I conduct evaluating interpersonal efforts:

1. Identify Key Network Contacts

I systematically review networking spheres, mapping individuals who have recently been elevated through deeper dialogue, perhaps nonprofit Executive Directors, corporate decision-makers, or influencers within the communities served.

I summarize brief biographies, noting first meeting moments, common passions discussed, or mutual support extended along our journeys. Then, I set calendar reminders quarterly to touch base genuinely beyond surface leveraging needs.

An example a network map might feature:

Alisha, Executive Director at Local Charity for Families
- Met at a fundraising gala last Fall

- Discovered we share a passion for eradicating child poverty and promoting economic mobility for families.

- Offers I provided: Hosting tables at fundraising breakfasts and connecting her to others who also share this passion.

Rahib, VP of Acquisitions at a Real Estate Equity Firm
- Serendipitously sat together at a couple of networking events

- Found we're both avid about redeveloping historical neighborhoods and housing justice.

- Followed up by linking his team to a friend's development portfolio for collaboration.

The key is staying organized about influencers in spheres of interest and nurturing affinity through continual engagement or quantified support exchange.

[Image: A vision board filled with personal and professional goals achieved through improved communication skills]

2. Reflect On Relational Improvements

I monitor my relationships' progress, noting the subtle shifts and deeper connections that result from being intentionally vulnerable, giving thoughtful gifts, embracing each other's love languages, reminiscing about the good old days, or offering genuine encouragement when I see growth.

Did our bonds strengthen because we consistently scheduled quality time together? Maybe those monthly homemade dinners led to reconciling differences or processing past traumas in a safe and comforting environment. Are our dreams starting to bloom because we're holding each other accountable in our careers or spiritual journeys?

I make sure to celebrate even the small milestones. Strong relationships aren't built overnight but through years of consistent effort and compassionately prioritizing each other.

3. List Professional Possibilities

Keep an ongoing list where your sharpened schmoozing and chatting skills have unlocked career opportunities you couldn't access before. Reflect on how courage and improved communication have opened doors previously closed to you.

Maybe your bravery in engaging with executives led to increased visibility and a leadership role. Or perhaps practicing public speaking boosted your confidence, enabling you to present deliverables to wide audiences and rapidly elevate your expertise and authority. Sharing past struggles might have quickly built bonds within niche industry networks, leading to collaborations that once seemed impossible when you kept hardships to yourself.

Our interpersonal efforts plant seeds that will eventually lead to abundant business bounties. Don't wait until the harvest to stay motivated—keep a list to remind yourself of the benefits of consistent interaction efforts today.

Maintaining motivation in mastering these skills comes from acknowledging courage and celebrating small progress points, no matter how modest. Celebrate these small wins and sustain your skills through continuous community engagement. Higher heights will unveil themselves unexpectedly over time. Onward and upward, my friends!

Conclusion

CONCLUSION: THE ART OF Connection

As we reach the final chapter of our journey through "Mastering Small Talk: Building Confidence and Strategies for Engaging Conversations," let's take a moment to reflect on the transformative power of meaningful connections. This book has been more than just a guide—it's been an invitation to unlock the potential within every conversation and to see small talk not as a chore, but as an art form that can enhance every aspect of our lives.

Reflecting on the Journey

When we first began, many of us viewed small talk as a daunting challenge, maybe even a necessary evil. But look at how far we've come! With the tools and techniques, you've learned, small talk has transformed from something to be avoided into a gateway for deeper connections and countless opportunities.

We discovered that small talk isn't about impressing others with witty remarks or profound insights. It's about creating a space where genuine human connection can flourish. By demonstrating sincere interest, actively listening, and responding thoughtfully, we've learned to turn even the briefest interactions into meaningful exchanges.

You've developed a robust set of skills—from mastering the art of initiating conversations to interpreting the subtle social cues that guide us through complex social landscapes. You've come to appreciate the power of open-ended questions, the importance of empathy, and the impact of nonverbal communication.

Your Next Steps: Keeping the Momentum Going

As you close this book, remember that mastering small talk is an ongoing journey. Like any other skill, it requires consistent practice and refinement. But the rewards—deeper relationships, expanded opportunities, and increased self-confidence—are well worth the effort.

Creating Your Personal Growth Plan

To help you continue on this path, I encourage you to create a personalized action plan. Here's a simple framework to get you started:

1. **Weekly Practice Goal:** Commit to initiating small talk in at least three new situations each week. This could be with a stranger in line at the coffee shop, a colleague you don't know well, or even a family member you'd like to connect with more deeply. (Choose a number that resonates with you, and increase it over time as you grow more comfortable.)

2. **Skill Focus:** Each month, select one specific skill from the book to concentrate on. Perhaps it's asking more open-ended questions or enhancing your non-verbal communication. Make this skill your focal point in interactions throughout the month.

3. **Reflection Journal:** Keep a small notebook or use a notes app on your phone to jot down your thoughts after conversations. What went well? What could be improved? What did you learn about the other person—or yourself?

4. **Feedback Loop:** Don't hesitate to ask trusted friends or family members for honest feedback on your conversational skills. Their insights can be incredibly valuable as you continue to grow.

5. **Stretch Goals:** Challenge yourself to step outside your comfort zone. If you've mastered small talk in casual settings, try applying your skills at a professional networking event. If you're comfortable one-on-one, practice in group settings.

Final Thoughts: Embrace the Power of Connection

Mastering small talk is about more than just making conversation—it's about creating meaningful connections that can enrich every aspect of your life. So keep practicing, keep growing, and remember that each conversation is an opportunity to learn, connect, and make a positive impact.

You've equipped yourself with the knowledge and strategies to thrive in any social situation. Now, go out there and let your words—and your presence—create ripples of connection wherever you go.

Final Reflections & Practice

1. REFLECT ON YOUR Progress:

Take a moment to remember where you were when you first picked up this book. How have your feelings about small talk changed? In what ways have you grown? Write down three specific improvements you've noticed in your conversational abilities.

2. Set Future Goals for Continued Growth:

Looking ahead, what aspects of your small talk skills would you like to develop further? Set three concrete goals for the next six months. For example, "I will initiate conversations with five new people at the next company event" or "I will practice using humor appropriately in my daily interactions with colleagues."

3. Encouragement and Final Thoughts

As we conclude our journey together, I want to leave you with a final thought. Small talk, at its core, is about human connection. Connecting genuinely with others is more valuable than ever in a world that often feels increasingly divided and isolated.

Every time you engage in small talk, you're not just passing the time or being polite. You're creating a moment of shared humanity, opening a door to understanding, empathy, and connection. In that light, small talk isn't small at all—it's the foundation of our social fabric.

So, the next time you find yourself in an elevator with a stranger, waiting in line at the grocery store, or at a social gathering where you don't know anyone, remember that you can create a moment of connection. You have the skills to turn that small talk into something meaningful.

Go forth with confidence, curiosity, and compassion. Every conversation is an opportunity to learn, grow, and make the world a little warmer and more connected. You've got this!

Thank you for joining me on this journey of mastering small talk. Here's to many engaging conversations and meaningful connections in your future!

About the Author

Meet Judy Best, the island-dwelling, dream-chasing, small talk enthusiast!

For over 40 years, Judy has been the reigning queen of her household, guiding two amazing kids into adulthood and now spoiling two grandkids with endless beach days and tropical adventures. A few years back, Judy and her husband decided to swap the mainland hustle for the serene sands of Puerto Rico, turning their dream into a vibrant reality that their family can't get enough of.

With a business management degree under her belt, Judy crushed it in the corporate world before ditching the 9-to-5 grind to dive into entrepreneurship. Now, she and her husband juggle a thriving real estate investment portfolio and a successful IT managed services company—because why stop at one empire when you can build two?

As a child, Judy would confidently declare, "I'm going to write books when I grow up!" And guess what? She wasn't kidding. This book is the first of many dreams coming true, and she's thrilled to share it with you.

Need a little nudge to master small talk and networking? You're in luck! Swing by JudyBest.com to connect with Judy, where you'll find the support and accountability you need to crush your goals. Plus, don't forget to snag the companion workbook to help you ace the Practice and Meditations in this book.

Let's turn those daydreams into reality together—because if Judy can do it, so can you!

Made in the USA
Monee, IL
08 September 2024